D0682768

Bloomsbury
Good Reading Guide
to Science Fiction
and Fantasy

Bloomsbury
Good Reading Guide
to Science Fiction
and Fantasy

M.H. ZOOL

BLOOMSBURY

First published 1989

Copyright ® Iffley Road Science Fiction Association

10   9   8   7   6   5   4   3   2   1

British Library Cataloguing in Publication Data
A CIP catalogue record for this book
is available from the British Library

ISBN   0 7475 0387 7

Designed by Malcolm Smythe
Typeset by Rapid Communications Ltd., London WC1
Printed in Great Britain by
Richard Clay Ltd, Bungay, Suffolk

Contents

Introduction

Science fiction, so long dismissed as nothing more than cliché in space, has over recent years begun to receive far greater popular and critical acceptance. Though the fans who remember when reading *Amazing Stories* was a secretive, shameful pleasure may complain that this has taken the fun out of sf, and the tightly-knit camaraderie out of sf fandom, most people are pleased that the genre is attracting more demanding readers and thoughtful writers. The scope of sf has never been broader: to the scientific interests of the Golden Age, New Wave writers added freedom of both style and subject matter, and authors of the past decade have reaped the benefits. Although anyone who has ever entered a bookshop to be faced with six shelves of Tolkien imitators might not appreciate the point, fantasy has developed alongside sf and many fine genre novels fall between the two camps. At the same time, mainstream writers have continued to turn to science fiction – sometimes even acknowledging the fact – to deal with issues the realistic tradition is not equipped to handle.

Certainly no one can now claim that sf is devoid of merit. But those who are intrigued by the genre and would like to dip into it are still faced with shelves of gaudy covers and gee-whiz blurbs. How, then, is one to separate the good from the bad? Where can those who develop a taste for sf find other books they might enjoy?

This *Guide* offers answers to those questions. It is not a work of literary criticism; I have come to recommend authors, not to bury them, and have therefore emphasised their strengths rather than criticised their weaknesses. Nor is it a reference book; for instance, I have only credited authors as short story writers when their short story output is worth mentioning. Moreover, it takes a purely sf angle on authors. I have not attempted to do justice to such literary titans as, say, ▷ Borges, ▷ Kafka or ▷ William Burroughs, but have been content to indicate their work's connections with the genre. My intention was to draw attention to books which will be enjoyed by sf readers, and to sf books which will be enjoyed by those meeting the genre for the first time.

Inevitably, a book like this reflects the prejudices and preferences of its writers. This is not necessarily a bad thing. It must also, however, reflect their limitations. I think that between me I have covered the field fairly comprehensively. Nevertheless, I am open to corrections, suggestions and reminders of things I have missed, particularly for follow-ups, skeins and menus.

Finally, I would like to dedicate this book to my parents. All thirty-eight of them.

M H ZOOL
Oxford, 1989

Acknowledgements

Many people contributed material to this book and limbs to its author. They are, in alphabetical order, Tim Adye, Matt Bishop, John Bray, Malcolm Cohen, Adrian Cox, Paul Cray, Melanie Dymond, John Grandidge, Graham Harper, Penny Heal, Mo Holkar, Paul Marrow, Jane McCarthy, Marina McDonald, Simon McLeish, Phil Raines, Robert Sadler, Ivan Towlson and Neal Tringham. The editors would like to thank Sian Facer, Colin Johnson, Jen McGowan, Kenneth McLeish and Kathy Rooney, who repaired things (eg sentences) for us. We also acknowledge debts to Peter Nicholls' *Encyclopedia Of Science Fiction* and Curtis Smith's *Twentieth Century Science Fiction Writers*, our main resources for names and dates when primary sources were not available.

The *Guide* was compiled by John Bray (menu collation), Mo Holkar (general editing), Ivan Towlson (general editing, technical co-ordination, liaison) and Neal Tringham (general editing, revision and replacement of entries, assistance with menus).

Glossary

Android   Human-shaped organic robot.

Cybernetics   A science concerned with the comparative study of automatic control systems (e.g. the nervous system and brain and a mechanical control system). Intricate objects can be made to act like living beings.

Cyberpunk   As exemplified by ▷ William Gibson, ▷ Bruce Sterling and their numerous imitators, cyberpunk envisages a sleazy, high-tech future, featuring a projection of our own society and culture rather than a single radical change. Gibson's *Neuromancer* is the seminal cyberpunk novel; Sterling's anthology *Mirrorshades* is an excellent survey of the field.

Cyborg   Part machine, part living being.

Fandom   This refers to a body of sf readers who are more active about their interest than just buying a book now and then. Many fans produce amateur magazines, and many more attend the science fiction conventions held with increasing frequency in most parts of the country. 'Fandom' is an informal grouping, but those interested in finding out more might wish to contact the British Science Fiction Association: for membership details write to Joanne Raine, 33 Thornville Rd, Hartlepool, Cleveland TS26 8EW.

Geosynchronous   A satellite is moving in a geosynchronous orbit if it remains above the same point on the Earth's surface at all times.

Golden Age   The term is used here to refer to the late 1930s and 40s, the heyday of John W Campbell's *Astounding* magazine, and of such authors as ▷ Isaac Asimov, ▷ Robert A Heinlein and ▷ Eric Frank Russell.

Hive-mind   Collective mind formed by several individuals, each usually significantly less intelligent than the *gestalt*; the name derives from the analogy to a beehive.

New Wave   The British New Wave was a revolution in sf style and content that took place in the 1960s largely thanks to ▷ Michael Moorcook's *New Worlds* magazine. The movement emphasised literary values, encouraged experimentation, and blew away many sf's longest-standing taboos. See also the entries for ▷ J G Ballard and ▷ William Burroughs.

   The American New Wave was a somewhat watered-down equivalent, much trumpeted by Harlan Ellison in his *Dangerous Visions* anthologies. Although it injected a lot of new blood into the stagnating American sf scene, much of it was essentially a re-run of the tamer experiments of the *New Worlds* writers. ▷ Samuel Delany was one of the best authors to emerge from this period. For a reading list, see the menu *The New Wave(s)*.

Psionics/psi powers   Super-normal mental powers such as telepathy, telekinesis or mind control.

Pulp   The style of fiction published by the 1920s and 30s magazines printed on pulp paper. Pulp fiction was often formulaic but offered room for considerable creativity within its mix of action, suspense and romance – as witness the best of pulp authors, such as ▷ Edgar Rice Burroughs.

Symbiosis   The living together of two dissimilar beings in a mutually beneficial relationship.

Symbiote   A being living in symbiosis.

Telepath   A being capable of telepathy, ie direct mind-to-mind communication of one sort or another.

How to use this book

Author Entries.   Each author entry contains some or all of four elements: a paragraph describing the author's work in general terms, sometimes by featuring a selection of books; a more detailed description of one book as a good example of the writer's work; a selection of the author's other books; and a list of suggested follow-ups. The latter are identified by the following symbols:

● further books by the same author
▶ by different authors
◊ directs you to a menu which we consider to be the best source of follow-ups.

Authors' birth/death dates and publication dates have been given where possible.

Menus.   There are over fifty menus scattered through the book. They suggest some of the classic, best and more representative books on particular themes or of particular types. We have also included menus of the Hugo and Nebula award winners, as explained under those entries.

Skeins.   Each skein begins with one book, and draws out a number of themes, each of which provides a list of follow-ups.

Glossary.   We have tried to make this wide-ranging enough to clarify even the jargon not used in the present volume.

Index.   The index is a valuable source of follow-ups. Many of our suggestions run both ways, but we have only listed one direction. To trace such references backwards, use the index to look up all of the entries in which the book you have enjoyed is mentioned.

Notation.   Throughout the book, the symbol ▷ next to a name indicates that the *Guide* contains an entry devoted to that author.

A

ADAMS, Douglas (born 1952)
British novelist and scriptwriter

In 1978 a series called *The Hitch-Hiker's Guide To The Galaxy* began on BBC Radio 4, involving among other things the total destruction of the Earth, the drinking habits of Betelgeusian journalists and a bewildered Earthman whose modest aim in life was to obtain a drinkable cup of tea from a vending machine. It went on to spawn a set of records and an official towel, not to mention four novels (*The Hitch-Hiker's Guide To The Galaxy; The Restaurant At The End Of The Universe; Life, The Universe And Everything; So Long And Thanks For All The Fish*, 1979–84). While Adams has perhaps overworked his initial idea, the first two books at least are brilliantly surreal off-the-wall comedies, loaded with catch-phrases, one-liners and side-swipes at terrestrial bureaucracy, pettiness and stupidity. *Dirk Gently's Holistic Detective Agency* (1987) is as episodic as the *Hitch-Hiker* series, but has a less convoluted style. When computer scientist Richard MacDuff is accused of murdering his boss, psychic eye Dirk undertakes to investigate the relationship of Richard's predicament to 'the fundamental interconnectedness of all things' – the things in question including a time-travelling professor, a horse, an Electric Monk and several pizzas. *The Long Dark Tea-Time Of The Soul* (1988) is the sequel.

READ·ON

- The original radio scripts, telling a different version of the *Hitch-Hiker's* story, have also been published.
- ▶ ▷ Harry Harrison, *The Technicolor Time Machine*
- ▷ John Sladek, *The Reproductive System*
- ▷ Terry Pratchett, *The Colour Of Magic*
- ▷ Bob Shaw, *Who Goes Here?*
- ▷ Robert Sheckley, *Dimension Of Miracles*
  Robert Rankin, *The Brentford Trilogy*

ALDISS, Brian (born 1925)
British novelist, short story writer and critic

Although the ambitious intentions of Aldiss' works are often weakened by lack of intensity, they remain among the most varied in the sf field. Metaphysical and ontological interests inform the bizarre time travel story *Cryptozoic!* (1967), *Report On Probability A* (a surreal story of a single suspended instant which collapses many worlds into one, 1968) and *Barefoot In The Head* (a Joycean account of a messiah to a Europe saturation-bombed with psychedelic drugs, 1969). Profound doubts about humanity's self-importance appear in *Hothouse* (1962: a brilliantly inventive story of a far-future Earth where tiny humans, their brains aided by symbiotic fungi, inhabit a continent-spanning tree) and *The Dark Light Years* (1964: about humanity's relations with a saintly alien race who wallow in excreta). *Trillion Year Spree* (1986) is an insightful if controversial history of sf, an entertaining and informative read. The 'Helliconia' trilogy (*Helliconia Spring, Summer* and *Winter*, 1982–85) describes a single cycle of the seasons on the planet of Helliconia – a cycle that takes several thousand years. The changing face of the world is grandly evoked, and mood and character are brilliantly handled.

READ·ON

● *Greybeard* (an atmospheric novel of a world where humanity has become sterile); *The Malacia Tapestry* (the richly evocative story of the beginnings of change in a changeless city); *Non-Stop*; *Enemies Of The System*; *The Saliva Tree* (stories).

▶ To *Helliconia*:
▷ Ursula K LeGuin, *The Left Hand Of Darkness*
▶ To *Barefoot In The Head*:
▷ J G Ballard, *The Atrocity Exhibition*
▶ To *The Malacia Tapestry*:
▷ M John Harrison, *In Viriconium*

ALIENS AND ALIEN SOCIETIES
▷ Poul Anderson, *The People Of The Wind*
▷ C J Cherryh, *The Faded Sun: Kesrith*
▷ Hal Clement, *Cycle Of Fire*
▷ Mary Gentle, *Golden Witchbreed*
▷ Ursula K LeGuin, *The Word For World Is Forest*
▷ Larry Niven, *Protector*
▷ Jack Vance, *City Of The Chasch*
Stanley Weinbaum, *A Martian Odyssey*
▷ H G Wells, *The First Men In The Moon*

ALTERNATE WORLDS/MULTIPLE REALITIES
Hawthorne Abendsen, *The Grasshopper Lies Heavy*
▷ Philip K Dick, *The Man In The High Castle*
▷ Harry Harrison, *A Transatlantic Tunnel, Hurrah!*
▷ Ursula K LeGuin, *The Lathe Of Heaven*
Richard Lupoff, *Circumpolar!*

H Beam Piper, *Lord Kalvan of Otherwhen/Gunpowder God*
▷ Keith Roberts, *Pavane*
▷ Robert Anton Wilson, *Schrödinger's Cat*
▷ Roger Zelazny, *Nine Princes In Amber*

ANDERSON, Poul (born 1926)
US novelist and short story writer

Anderson's primary talents have always lain with the depiction of doomed empires and unavoidable tragedies, in a universe where all morality is painted in bleak and shifting shades of grey. His characteristics as a writer are those of the romantic: a certain weakness with realistic characterisation, the ability to produce genuinely poetic prose, a tendency to turn dialogue into dramatic speeches. (*The Enemy Stars*, 1959, *The People Of The Wind*, 1973, *The Broken Sword*, 1954, and the novella of divided loyalties 'No Truce With Kings' are among his best romantic works, resembling ▷ Moorcock's *Stormbringer*). Anderson's other strengths include broad farce (*The Makeshift Rocket*, 1962) and stories centred around problems of alien psychology or biology. The best of the latter, involving much interesting speculation, are *The Man Who Counts* (1958) and the 1964 collection *Trader To The Stars*. *A Knight Of Ghosts And Shadows* (1974) is part of Anderson's series about Dominic Flandry, who struggles endlessly to preserve the decadent interstellar empire he serves because he realises that its inevitable successor will be total barbarism. In this novel Flandry is brought to what is perhaps his final understanding of his own nature; he is a soldier fighting a shadow war in which both he and his enemy can inflict terrible injuries upon each other in the name of causes in which neither of them truly believe.

READ·ON
● *The Best Of Poul Anderson* (collection)
▶ Other 'problem stories'
▷ Larry Niven, *Tales Of Known Space*
▷ Hal Clement, *Cycle Of Fire*
Colin Kapp, *The Unorthodox Engineers*

ANTHONY, Piers (born 1934)
US novelist and short story writer

Anthony's early novels include several works of serious sf. *Chthon* (1967) explores an essentially sado-masochistic male-female relationship within its story of a man's escape from a terrifying prison planet. The Omnivore trilogy (*Omnivore*, *Orn* and *Ox*, 1968–76) is concerned initially with alien perspectives on Earth ecology and later with interestingly detailed reptilian and mechanical intelligent inhabitants of parallel worlds. Later stories are more light-hearted, amusing adventures in a wide variety of settings. The Cluster novels, beginning with *Cluster* (1977), are space opera with a psychic slant, while *On A Pale Horse* (first of the Incarnations of Immortality series, 1985) is set on a parallel Earth where magic functions in an intriguingly novel fashion. The Xanth series (starting with *A Spell for Chameleon,* 1977) are enjoyably whimsical fantasies with a sentimental tinge, featuring such punning inventions as a magical Talent for the physical throwing of tantrums – invisible, but terribly painful to the victim. *Macroscope* (1969) is a complex but not too serious space opera. Its ingredients include a genetically improved superman, an alien signal which drives humans mad, and the planet Neptune used as a spaceship; its writing is enriched by large doses of psychology and astrology.

READ•ON

● *Sos The Rope* (post-holocaust adventure)
  Split Infinity (mingling fantasy and sf)
  Mute (revolution by underdog mutants)
▶ To Anthony's fantasy:
  ▷ Alan Dean Foster, *Spellsinger*
▶ To *Macroscope*:
  ▷ Robert Sheckley, *The Alchemical Marriage Of Alastair Crompton*
  Spider Robinson, *Callahan's Crosstime Saloon*

ASIMOV, Isaac (born 1920)
US writer of novels, short stories and non-fiction

Asimov, a child of John W Campbell Jr's Golden Age (a revolution in the American genre magazines which concentrated on the 'problem solving' aspect of sf) wrote many stories typical of the movement (collected in *The Early Asimov,* 1972, the superior *Nightfall,* 1969, and *Nine Tomorrows,* 1959); they rely for effect on a scientific idea or sting in the tail. 'Nightfall' itself, for example, describes the madness and horror experienced by the inhabitants of a world to which night comes for the first time in thousands of years. Later work shows Asimov developing and improving on this pattern, in stories that emphasize plotting and ideas above characterisation and style; they are generally based around some puzzle that must be solved, explicitly so in the Elijah Bailey series (*The Caves Of Steel, The Naked Sun,* and *The Robots Of Dawn,* 1954–84), ingenious detective stories set in a highly technological future. Among the features of this future are the famous 'Three Laws of Robotics', a set of basic instructions for robots designed to ensure they remain safe and useful, and also used as the basis for the short stories in the collection *The Complete Robot* (1982). Most famous of all Asimov's works is the Foundation trilogy (*Foundation, Foundation and Empire* and *Second*

Foundation, 1951–53), chronicling the fall of a moribund Galactic Empire and its replacement by the Foundation, aided by the dead hand of its founder who has predicted the future of the galaxy through scientific analysis of society.

THE GODS THEMSELVES (1972)

This is the story of the discovery of the 'positron pump' – a device which allows humanity to suck apparently unlimited energy from a parallel universe inhabited by aliens (who for their own reasons fail to warn humanity that continued use of the pump will destroy the Solar System). While the detailed pictures Asimov draws of the human scientists and society on the moon hold our interest, it is the section told from the point of view of the aliens, some of the most unusual (and convincing) in sf, which makes this book genuinely original. Subject to the different physical laws of the parallel universe, they are able to 'melt' into rocks and even each other – the basis for their intriguing tri-sexuality.

Asimov's short story collections include The Bicentennial Man, Earth Is Room Enough, *and* Asimov's Mysteries *(sf detective stories). The novels* The Stars Like Dust, The Currents Of Space, *and* Pebble In The Sky *are enjoyable tales of galactic intrigue. The Foundation series is continued, rather less credibly, in* Prelude To Foundation, Foundation's Edge *and* Foundation And Earth, *and linked to the Elijah Bailey novels by (inevitably)* Robots And Empire.

READ•ON

- ● *The End Of Eternity* (about the moral and psychological problems facing the members of an organisation which 'improves' human history to achieve the greatest good of the greatest number).
- ▶ To *The Complete Robot*:
  - ▷ Arthur C Clarke, *2001*; the intelligent computer, HAL, is supposed to follow Asimov's robot laws, until things go wrong . . .
- ▶ To *The Gods Themselves*:
  - ▷ Gregory Benford, *Timescape*
- ▶ To the detective stories:
  Agatha Christie, *Murder On The Orient Express*
- ▶ ▷ James Blish, *Cities In Flight*
  - ▷ Frederik Pohl, *Gateway*
  - ▷ Joe Haldeman, *Mindbridge*
- ▶ To the short stories:
  - ▷ Robert A Heinlein, *The Menace From Earth*
- ◊ Detective SF

Isaac ASIMOV • *Foundation*

▷ E E 'Doc' SMITH
FIRST LENSMAN
(a cosmic battle over the fate of two galaxies whose course can be predicted millennia ahead)

▷ Poul ANDERSON
THE BROKEN SWORD
(the preordained doom of a hero in a magical version of early Britain)

Fate And Prediction

▷ Robert SILVERBERG
THE STOCHASTIC MAN
(a study of contrasting attitudes to the power of precognition)

▷ Michael MOORCOCK
THE HIGH HISTORY OF THE RUNESTAFF
(the mystical Runestaff manipulates its chosen heroes to bring about the defeat of the Dark Empire of Granbretan)

▷ Kurt VONNEGUT
SLAUGHTERHOUSE-5
(Billy Pilgrim discovers the illusory nature of free will and learns to accept it in peace)

▷ Charles SHEFFIELD
BETWEEN THE STROKES OF NIGHT
(about people who perceive time at a very slow rate)

▷ Joe HALDEMAN
THE FOREVER WAR
(soldiers return from war to find Earth changed beyond recognition)

Long Time Scales

▷ Doris LESSING
SHIKASTA
(Earth, from primeval Eden to the present, seen as an episode in the colonial history of a galactic empire)

▷ Olaf STAPLEDON
LAST AND FIRST MEN
*(humanity: from our present form, to
extinction on Neptune millions of years
hence)*

Robert SHEA and ▷ Robert Anton
WILSON
ILLUMINATUS!
*(psychedelic fantasy of ancient conspiracies
battling to take over the world, or not)*

G K CHESTERTON
THE MAN WHO WAS THURSDAY
*(good citizen plans to spy on conspiracy,
only to discover the awful secret of the
conspirators' true identities . . .)*

Secret Societies

▷ Philip José FARMER
THE DARK DESIGN
*(the third 'Riverworld' book, in which the
resurrectees find themselves embroiled in
the rivalry between the resurrectors but
aren't sure exactly how)*

▷ Philip K DICK
RADIO FREE ALBEMUTH
*('Aramchek', led by an extraterrestrial
satellite, plots the destruction of the US
President)*

ASPRIN, Robert L (born 1946)
US novelist and short story writer

Asprin is best known for his Myth fantasy comedy series (including *Another Fine Myth, Myth Conceptions,* and *Myth Directions,* 1978 onward). The main characters are Skeeve, an archetypal slow-on-the-uptake magician's apprentice, and Aahz, a green scaly demon who has lost his powers due to a practical joke. The first three books in particular make light but very entertaining reading: fast paced, hilarious, not over-reliant on simple puns. Asprin also co-edits the serious fantasy series *Thieves' World,* in which guest authors write linked stories set in a common locality.

R E A D • O N ► To *Thieves' World:*
▷ Fritz Leiber, *The Swords Of Lankhmar*
► ▷ Terry Pratchett, *The Colour Of Magic*
Steven Brust, *To Reign In Hell*

ATWOOD, Margaret (born 1939)
Canadian novelist, short story writer, poet and critic

The Handmaid's Tale (1986) is the compelling account of a future American society of fundamentalist Christians, where fertile women become breeding stock and rapists are brutally executed. The atmosphere of a savage, claustrophobic society is portrayed with an impressive eye for detail, and the characters (male as well as female) are drawn with sympathy and an excellent sense of balance. An 'historical' afterword distances us from this horrific vision, allowing us to put it in perspective as a terrible warning.

R E A D • O N ● *Bluebeard's Egg* (non-sf collection)
► ▷ Keith Roberts, *Kiteworld*
◊ Feminism

B

BALLARD, J(ames) G(raham) (born 1930)
British novelist and short story writer

Ballard has said that science fiction is the true literature of the twentieth century, showing us the present through a vision of the future. Throughout his work he is concerned with 'inner space' and the human mind, focusing on the inner landscape of frequently alienated and obsessed characters and on their relationship with the reality around them. Through his surreal and dislocated images, his intensely visual descriptions giving new life to the otherwise mundane, Ballard gives us a unique vision of the world. Such early books as *The Drowned World* (1962) and *The Crystal World* (1966), about the progressive crystallisation of time, are disaster novels in which the central character appears to somehow sympathise with the ongoing catastrophe. Later he turned to experimental writing, abandoning linear narrative in *The Atrocity Exhibition* (1970) to present a set of images of the times, of car crashes and dead astronauts, Ronald Reagan and John F Kennedy. *Crash* (1973) explores an obsession with the sexual implications of the car crash, following themes from *The Atrocity Exhibition,* while *High Rise* (1975) describes the breakdown of society in a modern tower block. The themes of the novels are explored in a different way in such short stories as 'The Voices Of Time', which describes time as a solid, visible aspect of reality (in *The Voices Of Time,* 1962), and 'The Terminal Beach', a surreally experimental view of the nuclear bomb (in *The Terminal Beach,* 1964).

THE DAY OF CREATION (1988)

In the small African town of Port-la-Nouvelle, caught in the centre of a war between guerillas and government troops, Dr Mallory drills for water, dreaming of a third Nile and a green Sahara. He sees a new river appear and becomes obsessed with it, viewing it as a part of himself, to be named after him, owned by him and eventually destroyed by him. Mallory travels up the river to its source, pursued by both government and guerilla forces, accompanied by a television documentary producer and a teenage girl whom he sees as the personification of the river. During the journey, Mallory comes to accept the producer's view of the river and to see their journey as a film. The river dies at the moment when Mallory finally reaches its source, and in a reversal of his original intentions he now waits in the hope that it will return.

Ballard's other novels include The Drought, Concrete Island *(a motorist is trapped on a motorway traffic island),* The Unlimited Dream Company *(a crashed pilot becomes a suburban god) and* Hello America *(explorers from Europe wander through an abandoned United States covered by desert). His short story collections include* Vermilion Sands *(surprisingly gentle stories of a future artists' colony),* The Disaster Area, Low-Flying Aircraft *and* Myths of the Near Future.

READ·ON
● *Empire Of The Sun* (a semi-autobiographical story of a young boy imprisoned by the Japanese, giving a personal perspective on the themes of Ballard's other work)

▶ ▷ William Burroughs, *The Soft Machine*
Bernard Wolfe, *Limbo 90*

▷ Franz Kafka, *The Trial*
▷ Barry Malzberg, *The Falling Astronauts*
   Anna Kavan, *Ice*
▷ Michael Moorcock ed, *New Worlds*
   Garry Kilworth, *Spiral Winds*
   Christine Brooke-Rose, *Out*

BANKS, Iain (born 1954)
British novelist

Banks burst onto the literary scene in 1984 with the delightfully graphic tale of an alienated, sadistic Scottish youth, *The Wasp Factory*. Banks' maniacal black humour, pacy writing and vivid imagery make the novel highly enjoyable, and it poses pointed questions about living under rigid and unnatural systems. *Walking On Glass* (1985) contains three interwoven narratives: the stories of lovelorn student Graham Park, of paranoid Steven Grout, and of Quiss, forced to play impossible games in a Gormenghast-like castle until he or his opponent can answer an insoluble riddle. Banks' best novel to date is *The Bridge* (1986), a many-levelled story investigating the unconscious mind of a car-crash victim. Most of the action takes place on a Kafkaesque nightmare-version of the Forth Bridge, where the crash actually occurs, but much of the book consists of digressions into the hero's dreams, his life story and a hilarious sword-and-sorcery parody. Banks' haunting imagery is imposing but oblique; the individual strands of the story are all memorable in themselves, and they mesh together, reflecting the bridges they describe, to form a masterpiece.

READ·ON

● *Consider Phlebas* and *The Player Of Games* are forays into genre sf. *Espedair Street* depicts the torment and frustration of an ageing rock star.

▶ To *The Wasp Factory*:
   Kathy Acker, *Don Quixote*
▷ J G Ballard, *Crash*
▷ Clive Barker, *The Damnation Game*.

▶ To *The Bridge*:
▷ Franz Kafka, *The Castle*
▷ Doris Lessing, *Briefing For A Descent Into Hell*
   Alasdair Gray, *Lanark*

BARKER, Clive (born 1952)
British short story writer and novelist

Barker's policy of 'showing the monster' gave Britain's tired horror industry a new lease of life. His writing in the six *Books Of Blood* collections (1984–5) is vivid and poetic, and his ability to communicate fear is rarely rivalled. His talent for strong images produces stories like 'In The Hills, The Cities', in which two rural towns meet in murderous ritual combat, their people stacked into two vast human forms. *The Damnation Game* (1985) is Barker's first attempt at a horror novel, and *Weaveworld* (1987) combines his usual interests with a fantasy narrative.

R E A D • O N
- ▶ Ramsey Campbell, *Dark Feasts*
- ▷ George R R Martin ed, *Night Visions*
- ▷ William Burroughs, *The Naked Lunch*
- ▶ To *Weaveworld*:
  Michael Ende, *The Neverending Story*

BARTH, John (born 1931)
US novelist and short story writer

Barth's only sf novel is the mammoth *Giles Goat-Boy* (1966), which describes the coming of a Christ figure to an analogue of 1960s America. The world-as-university metaphor, though occasionally laboured, provides an ideal context for Barth to tell the story of the would-be Grand Tutor's reception, education and ultimate rejection. The novel is remarkable for the way its multifarious ancillary themes illuminate the central story, and for its speculative, unexpected connection between virgin birth and the Oedipus myth.

R E A D • O N
- ● *The Sot-Weed Factor; Chimera*
- ▶ ▷ Robert A Heinlein, *Stranger In A Strange Land*
- ▷ Gene Wolfe, *The Book Of The New Sun* uses similar messianic themes – but from Revelation, rather than the Gospels.

BAYLEY, Barrington J(ohn) (born 1937)
British novelist and short story writer

Bayley uses the space opera form to present impressively complex and original ideas, embedded within a simple action adventure narrative. *Collision With Chronos* (1973), for example, postulates that consciousness is associated with the present 'now', and that 'now' can move in different directions in different places, leading to collisions between lines of temporal flow. *The Soul*

Of The Robot (1974), set on a far-future Earth, speculates on the differences between a truly 'conscious' being and a mechanical imitation.

READ·ON   ●   *The Zen Gun* (featuring an ultimate weapon carved from wood)
                        The Fall Of Chronopolis
                        The Knights Of The Limits (collection)
       ▶ ▷   Iain Banks, *The Player Of Games*
          ▷   R A Lafferty, *Fourth Mansions*

BEAGLE, Peter (born 1939)
US novelist

Beagle is one of the most literary of contemporary fantasy writers. *A Fine And Private Place* (1960) is a love story between ghosts, told in an elegant and sophisticated style anticipating ▷ John Crowley's *Little, Big*. *The Last Unicorn* (1968), his masterpiece, is the story of a unicorn who may or may not be the last of her species, Schmendrick, who is either an utter failure or the greatest magician remaining in the world, and the romantic pragmatist Molly. It is by turns moving, wistful and hilarious.

READ·ON   ●   *The Folk Of The Air*
       ▶ ▷   Lord Dunsany, *The Charwoman's Shadow*
          ▷   R A MacAvoy, *Tea With The Black Dragon*
              Richard Grant, *Saraband Of Lost Time*

BEAR, Greg (born 1951)
US novelist and short story writer

Bear's early work, including stories such as 'The Venging', in which a group of humans is trapped in an environment utterly without stimulus, and novels like *Beyond Heaven's River* (1980), is straightforward hard sf. His reputation depends almost entirely on his recent novels, each of which explores a millenarian vision of apocalypse or transformation. *Blood Music* (1986) describes the consequences of the creation of intelligent cells by Vergil Ulam, an interestingly drawn biologist, as a private research project. Unwilling to turn them over to his company, he is forced to smuggle them out of the laboratory in his own bloodstream – but they escape into the environment, eventually converting the entire population of the US into one sentient protoplasmic mass. *The Forge Of God* (1987) begins with the disappearance of Jupiter's moon Europa and works up to the spectacular destruction of the planet Earth. *Eon* (1985) is a superb piece of hard sf, with all its characteristic faults and virtues. In our near future, a self-propelled asteroid approaches Earth from beyond the Solar System. Investigators discover that it is from Earth's future – but an alternate Earth's. Despite uncertain direction and weak characterisation, the novel is full of fascinating scientific ideas: prosthetic personalities, artificial emotions and the infinitely long seventh chamber of the asteroid, occupied by alien Jarts before it was built.

READ·ON   ● *The Infinity Concerto* and *The Serpent Mage* are musically based fantasy
▶ ▷ Bruce Sterling, *Schismatrix*
▷ Arthur C Clarke, *2001*
▷ Ian Watson, *The Jonah Kit*

BENFORD, Gregory (born 1941)
US novelist and short story writer

Benford is essentially a writer of ideas, which he explores in considerable – and yet always highly readable – technical detail. Such novels as *Timescape* (1980) also demonstrate a gift for perceptive characterisation; the book convincingly describes the people involved in a project to send messages back in time to warn the past about the chemical pollution which is destroying the future world. The imaginary physics of tachyon transmission and the details of scientific research are unfailingly credible and interesting. In *The Stars In Shroud* (1978), humanity is under attack by aliens using a psychological weapon. Benford's most recent book, *Great Sky River* (1987), is set in a far future world where enhanced humans are hunted by intelligent machines. *Across The Sea Of Suns* (1984) centres on the common Benford theme of conflict between organic beings and their cybernetic descendants. While an exploring starship finds lifeless worlds watched by orbiting machines, other mechanical intelligences fill Earth's oceans with hostile aliens. In Benford's universe, although organic life never manages to conquer its ancient enemy, it is never totally defeated, springing up wherever it can.

READ·ON   ● *In The Ocean Of Night* (the prequel to *Across The Sea Of Suns*)
If The Stars Are Gods (with Gordon Eklund)
Against Infinity (Ganymedean colonists confront the utterly alien)
In Alien Flesh (stories)
▶ To war with machines:
▷ Fred Saberhagen, *The Berserker Wars*
▶ ▷ Joe Haldeman, *The Forever War*
▷ Frederik Pohl, *Wolfbane*
▷ Bob Shaw, *A Wreath Of Stars*

BESTER, Alfred (1913–87)
US novelist and short story writer

Boundless energy and a furious rate of invention have always been Bester's trademarks. He has said that his writing obeys the old Hollywood injunction 'start with an earthquake and build to a climax', an accurate description except that it ignores the wit and irony which illuminate his prose. His short stories, collected in *Starlight* (1977), are intelligent and interesting, but his first real triumph was the novel *The Demolished Man* (1953). On one level this is a conventional sf detective story set in a vividly realised society containing many telepaths (whose presence makes a murderer's life extremely difficult); but it is also a Freudian study in guilt and obsessive hatred, told with considerable passion and many stylistic experiments. *Tiger! Tiger!/The Stars My Destination* (1956), his next novel, is the story of Gully Foyle, forced to unleash the furies of his inner nature by the refusal of a passing vessel to save him from the remains of a wrecked spaceship. Foyle releases untapped potentials of the human mind to take revenge on those who abandoned him, while in the background great powers manoeuvre to find a lost supply of the most dangerous substance in the solar system – themes that are triumphantly united at the novel's climax.

READ·ON

● *The Deceivers* (as inventive as the earlier books, if less coherent)

▶ ▷ Algis Budrys, *Rogue Moon*
  ▷ Henry Kuttner, *Fury*
  Alexandre Dumas, *The Count Of Monte Cristo*

BIG ENGINEERING PROJECTS
▷ James Blish, *Cities In Flight*
▷ Arthur C Clarke, *The Fountains Of Paradise*
▷ Larry Niven, *Ringworld*
▷ Terry Pratchett, *Strata*
▷ Bob Shaw, *Orbitsville*
▷ John Varley, *Titan*

BIO-ENGINEERING
  Kobo Abe, *Inter Ice-Age 4*
▷ Greg Bear, *Blood Music*
▷ James Blish, *The Seedling Stars*
▷ C J Cherryh, *Serpent's Reach*
▷ Frank Herbert, *The Eyes Of Heisenberg*
▷ Cordwainer Smith, *Norstrilia*

▷ Bruce Sterling, *Schismatrix*
▷ Kate Wilhelm, *Where Late The Sweet Birds Sang*

BISHOP, Michael (born 1945)
US novelist and short story writer

Bishop's novels are generally complex and occasionally abstruse; several feature the analysis of other cultures, on Earth in *Transfigurations* (1979) and *No Enemy But Time* (the story of a man who is sent back in time to become part of a tribe of *Homo habilis*, 1982) or on other planets in *A Funeral For The Eyes Of Fire* (1975). *Who Made Stevie Crye?* (1987), contrastingly, combines horror with fantasy in its hallucinatory tale of a writer's problems with her seemingly haunted typewriter.

READ · ON
●   *Ancient Of Days*
  Close Encounters With The Deity (mostly religious short stories)
  The Secret Ascension, Or Philip K Dick Is Dead, Alas
▶   To *No Enemy But Time*:
  William Golding, *The Inheritors*
▶   To *Who Made Stevie Crye?*:
▷   Christopher Priest, *The Affirmation*
◊   Aliens and Alien Societies

BLISH, James (1921–75)
US novelist, short story writer and critic

Blish's novels fall into two main categories: a large body of juvenile fiction (over a dozen *Star Trek* novelisations, plus books such as *The Star Dwellers,* 1961) and a smaller kernel of more complex works. His main preoccupations were with the ethical problems of the acquisition of knowledge (explored in *The Seedling Stars,* 1957, which deals with the physical alteration of humans to allow them to survive on alien worlds), and the possibility of a reconciliation between religion and science. The trilogy *After Such Knowledge* (1958–68), comprising *Doctor Mirabilis* (an historical novel about changing models of reality), *Black Easter,* and *A Case Of Conscience,* examines both of these themes with a thoughtful precision matched by few other authors. *A Case Of Conscience* is Blish's most powerful novel, a complex and convincing character study centred on the moral dilemmas of Ramon Ruiz-Sanchez, a priest and scientist who finds himself on Lithia, a planet which is literally paradise. He is forced to the conclusion that the planet is the creation of the devil – but to believe the devil capable of creation is heresy.

READ•ON
- Cities In Flight (describing humanity's expansion into the galaxy in mobile cities, employing the intriguingly peculiar physics of the anti-gravity spindizzy)
  Jack Of Eagles (an early novel of psionics)
  Galactic Cluster (collection)
▶ To A Case Of Conscience:
  ▷ Philip K Dick, The Transmigration Of Timothy Archer
▶ To The Seedling Stars:
  ▷ Frederik Pohl, Man Plus

BORGES, Jorge Luis (1899–1987)
Argentinian short story writer and poet

Borges' 'fictions' are models of economy: constructed with meticulous care, each conveys a remarkable breadth of knowledge, dry wit and lucidity of thought. *Labyrinths* (1964) anthologises his work admirably, covering the metaphysical, mathematical and literary sides of his writing. In these haunting, timeless stories, librarians seek God in an infinite, random universe-library; an imagined world gradually infects our own; and the absorbing, complex 'The Garden Of Forking Paths' seeks, characteristically, a single metaphor for time, literature and life.

READ•ON
- Six Problems For Don Isidro Parodi (with Adolfo Bioy Casares)
▶ ▷ Stanislaw Lem, A Perfect Vacuum
  Milan Kundera, The Book Of Laughter And Forgetting
  Alberto Manguel ed, Black Water

BOVA, Ben (born 1932)
US editor, novelist and short story writer

Best known as editor of the magazines *Analog* and *Omni,* and in this role highly influential in the development of sf since 1972, Bova has also written a number of novels and some shorter fiction. His books deal in traditional vein with speculative topics of hard or soft science; typical is *Millennium* (1976), a careful study of political interplay in the face of impending disaster. Bova's other titles include *The Dueling Machine* (1969), *The Weathermakers* (1967), *As On A Darkling Plain* (1972) and *The Multiple Man* (1976).

READ·ON
- Maxwell's Demons (collection)
- ▷ Orson Scott Card, Ender's Game
- ▷ Gregory Benford, Across The Sea Of Suns
- ▷ Algis Budrys, Michaelmas

BRADBURY, Ray (born 1920)
US novelist and short story writer

Fantastic images of 1950s America dominate Bradbury's fiction, which projects small-town characters and backgrounds on to other planets and into the future. His style is graphic and freely descriptive; he uses adjectives in abundance, occasionally in such quantities that they obscure the plot. Although many of his stories contain elements of horror, these are rarely overt, merely suggested by Bradbury's careful use of language; usually they contrast sharply with the essential benignity of his backdrops, and often with the innocence of his main characters as well. His short stories include 'The End Of The Beginning', in which parents worry over their spacefaring son, 'Dark They Were And Golden-Eyed', about Martian settlers from Earth who turn native (both in The Day It Rained Forever, 1959), and 'There Will Come Soft Rains', a moving story about a highly complex and almost intelligent house abandoned in the aftermath of a nuclear holocaust. The latter forms part of Bradbury's best-known collection, The Martian Chronicles/The Silver Locusts (1951), which traces twenty-five years of the history of our contact with Mars and with the enigmatic, elusive Martians who at first resist contact with humanity and then begin to merge with it. The stories in The Martian Chronicles carry with them a haunting sense of nostalgia and loss – a common theme in Bradbury's work, but rarely expressed as powerfully as here.

FAHRENHEIT 451 (1953)
Named for the temperature at which book paper ignites, this novel depicts a future society in which 'intellectual' has become an obscenity and books are considered fit only for destruction. Guy Montag is a fireman, one of the elite band who are called out to burn both illegally owned books and the houses which contain them. The firemen are revered by the adults who vegetate before the four-wall TV screens and by the children who find release in violence and destruction; they are reviled by the few who cling to their forbidden libraries. Montag commits the cardinal sin of reading one of the books he has been assigned to burn – and, for the first time, begins to doubt the vacuous society in which he lives. He steals some of the condemned volumes and secretes them at home, an action which can lead only to disaster. Fahrenheit 451 is a powerful demonstration of Bradbury's love of fantasy and his hatred of the antiseptic technocracy he thought was destroying it.

Bradbury's other works include the collections The Small Assassin, The Golden Apples Of The Sun *and* The Illustrated Man. *His novels include the episodic* Something Wicked This Way Comes *(a fantasy about a carnival of evil that comes to a small American town),* Dandelion Wine *and his most recent major work,* Death Is A Lonely Business, *though this owes more to horror than to fantasy.*

READ•ON
- ▶ Charles G Finney, *The Circus Of Dr Lao*
- ▷ Clifford Simak, *City*
- ▶ To *Something Wicked This Way Comes*:
  Tom Reamy, *Blind Voices*
  James P Blaylock, *The Land Of Dreams*
- ▶ To Bradbury's concern for the value of fantasy:
- ▷ George R R Martin, *Sandkings*
- ▷ Kurt Vonnegut, *Cat's Cradle*
- ▶ To his nostalgia:
- ▷ John Crowley, *Engine Summer*

BRADLEY, Marion Zimmer (born 1930)
US novelist and short story writer

On the planet Darkover, Bradley's most famous creation, conventional technology is at a medieval level, psionics instead being developed into a science, vividly portrayed in *Stormqueen!* (1978). Most of the books are, however, set much later, when most of the science has been destroyed in wars and the powers of those gifted with psionics resemble magic. The clash between the Terran Empire and its long-lost colony Darkover is a common theme, demonstrating how the technologically poorer society is not necessarily less cultured. *The Shattered Chain* (1976) contrasts female roles in the two societies and describes the 'Guild of Free Amazons', which provides support for women to live without dependence on men and is an anomaly in the patriarchal Darkovan society. Bradley has also written *The Mists Of Avalon* (1982), a detailed retelling of the Arthurian legend from the point of view of the women of the court, offering intriguing new perspectives on all aspects of the myth. *The Heritage Of Hastur* (1975) is one of the later Darkover books. It consists of the interlinked narratives of Lew Alton and Regis Hastur, heirs to their respective domains, and traces their fortunes when they become involved with a psychic rebellion. Culture clash between the Terran Empire and Darkover is a major theme of this book, emphasised through differences in their technology, sexuality and political freedom.

READ•ON
- ● *Sharra's Exile*
  Lythande (set in ▷ Asprin's *Thieves World*)

► ▷ Andre Norton, *Witch World*
▷ Katherine Kurtz, *The Legends Of Camber Of Culdi*
▷ Julian May, *The Many-Coloured Land*
▷ Anne McCaffrey, *Dragonflight*

BRIN, David (born 1950)
US novelist and short story writer

Brin is that rare thing in modern sf – an unrelentingly enthusiastic optimist. His writing takes an updated approach to the concerns of the 'Golden Age' of the 1940s, combining technology with neo-hippy concepts, poetry and puns with straightforward storytelling. His novels include the 'Uplift' series (*Sundiver, Startide Rising* and *The Uplift War*, 1987), set in a universe inhabited by a multitude of alien races, each of which has been 'uplifted' to an intelligent state by some previous race – except, apparently, for humanity. *The Practice Effect* (1984) is the light-hearted tale of an alternate world where things improve (rather than wear out) with use and pigs fly. In *The Postman* (1987), American civilisation has been destroyed by nuclear war, plagues and survivalist activity which also hampers any possible recovery. Gordon Krantz finds a postman's jacket and uses his acting skills to convince the next settlement that he is a courier of the 'Restored US'. The inhabitants, eager to believe him, give him letters to deliver, and his charade gathers force until the postal network he builds up eventually unites one single state: Oregon. Brin effectively brings home the fragility of the new state, as a survivalist attack almost destroys it, but the heart of the novel is his account of the power of popular belief, a provocative angle on myth and one rarely examined in sf.

READ·ON
● *The River Of Time* (collection)
► ▷ Roger Zelazny, *Doorways In The Sand*
▷ Bruce Sterling, *Schismatrix*
▷ Gordon R Dickson, *Way Of The Pilgrim*

BROWN, Fredric (1907–72)
US short story writer and novelist

Brown's best work consists of short-short stories: though his novels (of which the best is *What Mad Universe*, 1949) are entertaining, he really excelled at sketches and anecdotes. 'Answer', for instance, set up one of the enduring pulp images: the supercomputer which tells a theologically-minded questioner 'Yes . . . *now* there is a God.' His *Nightmare In . . .* stories are as neat and merciless as Roald Dahl's horror writing. *The Best Of Fredric Brown* is a fine collection.

READ•ON ● *Nightmares And Geezenstacks*
▶ For Brown's closest relation in the field of sf humour, ▷ Robert Sheckley, *The Robert Sheckley Omnibus*. For more short-short fiction, *100 Great Science Fiction Short Short Stories* edited by ▷ Asimov, Greenberg and Olander.
▶ Howard Waldrop, *Howard Who?*

BRUNNER, John (born 1934)
British novelist and short story writer

While Brunner has produced many enjoyable adventures and space operas, he is best known for his near-future dystopias. These combine interesting plots with vivid warnings of such dangers as overpopulation (*Stand On Zanzibar*, 1968), pollution (*The Sheep Look Up*, 1972), social decay (*The Jagged Orbit*, 1969) and over-rapid change (*The Shockwave Rider*, 1975). To describe life in such futures, Brunner weaves into the main narrative the unconnected stories of ordinary people, and makes frequent use of convincing and effectively deployed slang, quotations, newscasts, and even advertising. Although this makes the novels harder to get into, it is what brings their futures to vivid life. In the vastly overcrowded America of *Stand On Zanzibar,* social collapse is provoked by desperate governmental control of people's desire to procreate. Only the discovery of a surprisingly peaceful African tribe can prevent world-wide disaster, a perhaps too fantastic solution that nevertheless introduces an element of hope into one of sf's most thorough examinations of a dystopian future.

READ•ON ● *The Crucible Of Time* (about the development of science, quite different to our own, on another planet whose inhabitants are fired by the belief that they must leave their world or perish)
The Compleat Traveller in Black (fantasy moral tales of conflict against chaos)
The Squares of the City
▶ To *Stand On Zanzibar*:
▷ Harry Harrison, *Make Room! Make Room!*
▶ ▷ William Gibson, *Neuromancer*:
▷ James Blish and Norman L Knight, *A Torrent Of Faces*
Kevin O'Donnell, *ORA:CLE*

▶ To Brunner's 'documentary' technique:
   John Dos Passos, *USA*

BUDRYS, Algis (born 1931)
US novelist and short story writer

Though the quality of Budrys' work is now widely recognised, he remains one of the most underread writers of his generation, perhaps because his work is difficult to categorise. Such novels as *Rogue Moon* (1960) are full of profoundly resonant images: a death-obssessed adventurer's duplicates (created by a matter transmitter), sent to investigate a mysterious alien construct discovered on the moon, are killed by it one after another. In temporary telepathic contact with each of the replicas due to their near-exact physical similarity, the explorer suffers every one of their deaths. This book also showcases Budrys' talent for the sensitive characterisation of abnormal personalities – here the adventurer and the dedicated scientist who goads him into conquering the construct. Another such image is the charismatic news presenter of *Michaelmas* (1977), who secretly manipulates world affairs through his control of computer networks – and does so with sense and humanity. In *Who?* (1958) an American scientist is salvaged by the Russians after a laboratory explosion, and is returned to the West so thoroughly rebuilt that no-one can tell whether he is himself or a Soviet impostor. Using this device, the novel examines existential problems of identity, powerfully conveying the terror we feel at the idea of a man without a face – and the tragedy of his own inevitable loneliness.

READ·ON
● *The Iron Thorn* (a somewhat
   ▷ Sheckleyesque interplanetary adventure)
   Some Will Not Die (a grim tale of recovery
   from a catastrophic epidemic)
   Blood And Burning (collection)
▶ ▷ Alfred Bester, *Tiger! Tiger!*
   ▷ Robert Silverberg, *The Man In The Maze*
   ▷ Roger Zelazny, *Eye Of Cat*

BURGESS, Anthony (born 1917)
British novelist

Amongst Burgess's impressively diverse output are several works of sf. *A Clockwork Orange* (1962) is one of his most savage works; it is set in a dystopia where a brutal young thug is brainwashed into an aversion to violence – but with his criminality (and, we are made to feel, his free will) goes his essential humanity (as represented by his love of classical music). The story is told in a fascinating slang, made up of Burgess' original inventions and derivations from Russian. Burgess' other sf works are *The Wanting Seed, The End Of The World News* and *1985*.

READ•ON ► ▷ George Orwell, *1984*
► To the language:
Russell Hoban, *Riddley Walker*

BURROUGHS, Edgar Rice (1875–1950)
US novelist

'ERB's' talent was for fantastic, colourful adventure stories, with settings ranging from distant planets to the hollow centre of our own world. His stories glorify personal honour and formal romance, and are laced with satire and exotic (if unlikely) invention. If today his style seems old-fashioned and his characterisation and morality doubtful, his novels remain superb pieces of escapism. *A Princess Of Mars, Tarzan Of The Apes, At The Earth's Core* and *Pirates Of Venus* are the first books in each of his most famous series.

READ•ON ► Leigh Brackett, *The Sword Of Rhiannon*
▷ Lin Carter, *The Wizard Of Lemuria*
▷ Philip Jose Farmer, *Lord Tyger* is a realistic modern treatment of the Tarzan theme

---

BURROUGHS, William (born 1914)
US novelist

Burroughs was a powerful influence on the British New Wave movement of the 1960s. His major novels, such as *The Naked Lunch,* were written using a 'cut-up, fold-in' technique, in which the original text is cut into short sections which are then reassembled at random. This demands application on the part of the reader but communicates Burroughs' disjointed, hallucinatory world better than any simple description could. The explicit and occasionally sickening visions of homosexuality and drug abuse provide a horrifying metaphor for the perverted power relationships of modern society.

READ•ON ● *Cities Of The Red Night*
Nova Express
► Kathy Acker, *Blood And Guts In High School*
▷ J G Ballard, *Crash*
Hunter S Thompson, *Fear And Loathing In Las Vegas*

C

CABELL, James Branch (1879–1958)
American novelist

Cabell's chief fantasy interest lies in his bitter, sardonic investigations of godhead; in his work, creation is usually the result of boredom, and divine will is bureaucratically petty in application. His major achievement – mannered, witty, ironic and teasing – is the loosely linked series *The Descendants Of Dom Manuel*, featuring the ruler of the imaginary realm of Poictesme and twenty-three generations of his family. On this broad canvas Cabell studies the nature of heroic life via two protagonist types: the man of action, exemplified by Manuel in *Figures Of Earth* (1921), and the thinker-poet, such as the eponymous hero of *Jurgen* (1919).

R E A D • O N   ●   Other works include *The Silver Stallion, The High Place* and *The Line Of Love* (collection).
                ▶ ▷ Fritz Leiber, *The Swords Of Lankhmar*
                 ▷ Robert Sheckley, *Dimension Of Miracles*

ČAPEK, Karel (1890–1938)
Czech novelist and playwright

Čapek, an excellent satirist, is best known for the play *R.U.R./Rossum's Universal Robots* (1921), an allegory of worker/employer relations which gave us the word 'robot'. The androids (not ▷ Asimovian robots) work very well until they are given human emotions, which cause them to revolt and kill their creators. Čapek's novels are often funnier and vastly more original. They include *The Absolute At Large* (1922), about the terrifying consequences of the invention of a new energy source, and *War With The Newts* (1936), dealing with the discovery and exploitation of a race of intelligent newts.

R E A D • O N   ▶ ▷ Stanislaw Lem, *The Futurological Congress*
                 ▷ John Sladek, *Tik-Tok*
                 ▷ Robert Sheckley, *Journey Beyond Tomorrow*

CARD, Orson Scott (born 1951)
US novelist and short story writer

Card's work is unusually rich and wide-ranging: from the far-future technology of *Ender's Game* (1986) to the medieval atmosphere of *Hart's Hope* (1986), his settings are varied and his characters efficiently drawn. Such books as *Capitol* (1979), a collection of ingenious, powerful stories about the social effects of the suspended animation drug somec, *Wyrms* (1988) and the down-beat collection *Unaccompanied Sonata* (1983), which includes 'Closing The Timelid' and 'Mortal Gods', two widely differing examinations of death, have won him wide acclaim. With a sharp wit and a ready supply of ideas, Card's style is extremely readable; he introduces new concepts without fanfare and draws the reader effortlessly into believable societies. *Ender's Game* details the training of six-year-old Ender Wiggin in a futuristic military school. Isolated from his family on Earth, and from his colleagues at the school, Ender's only escape is brilliance. His brother and sister, rejected for this training, attempt to use propaganda to end the war. The three children are well-characterised; though the Battle School is extremely technological, its machines are not allowed to dominate the novel. The story of Ender and his sister Valentine is continued in *Speaker For The Dead* (1986), which explores the issues raised more deeply and in a less militaristic context.

READ·ON
- ● *Hot Sleep* (set in the universe of *Capitol*)
- ▶ To the Ender stories:
- ▷ Keith Roberts, *Molly Zero*
- ▷ James Blish, *A Case Of Conscience*
- ▶ To *Capitol*:
- ▷ Bob Shaw, *Other Days, Other Eyes*
- ▷ D G Compton, *The Continuous Katherine Mortenhoe*
- ▷ Cordwainer Smith, *The Rediscovery Of Man*

CARTER, Angela (born 1940)
British novelist and short story writer

Carter's fantasies are written in a very lucid style, laced with poetic imagery. Often, invention is used but sparingly and is the more effective for this. Indeed, *The Magic Toyshop* (1967) is almost completely a mainstream work, the magic lying not in impossible creations and events but rather in the exposition and development of its themes: coming of age, and love. Major topics of Carter's books are sexuality and social mores; this is seen most clearly in *The Passion Of New Eve* (1977), a powerful feminist fantasy set in a collapsing society of the near future.

READ·ON
- ● *Nights At The Circus* (an enchanting fantasy set at the turn of the century)
- ▶ ▷ Gwyneth Jones, *Divine Endurance*
- ▷ Tanith Lee, *Red As Blood*

CARTER, Lin (1930–1987?)
US novelist, short story writer and editor

Carter wrote a large quantity of popular fantasy, in subgenres ranging from Earthmen (never women) fighting for survival on alien planets (eg *Under The Green Star,* 1972) to scientific adventures set on our own world (such as *Zarkon, Lord Of The Unknown, In The Nemesis Of Evil,* 1975). The Thongor series, concerning the adventures of the northern barbarian Thongor on the exotic prehistoric island of Lemuria, typifies his work, resembling a head-on collision in writing style between ▷ Howard and ▷ E R Burroughs.

READ•ON   ● *Thongor In The City Of Magicians*
▶ Andrew Offutt with R Lyon, *Demon In The Mirror*
◊ Sword and Sorcery

CATASTROPHES
▷ J G Ballard, *The Crystal World*
▷ John Christopher, *The Death Of Grass*
▷ Richard Cowper, *The Twilight Of Briareus*
▷ Kurt Vonnegut, *Galapagos*
▷ John Wyndham, *The Day Of The Triffids*
Chelsea Quinn Yarbro, *Time Of The Fourth Horseman*

CHERRYH, C J (born 1942)
US novelist and short story writer

A focus on the society and culture of both humans and aliens characterises Cherryh's work, as in her *Faded Sun* trilogy, beginning with *Kesrith* (1978), which describes the conflicts between humans and two alien races during the establishment of peace after a long war. In *Serpent's Reach* (1979) she describes a mixed alien–human society where the aliens are hive minds. The human side of this society is split into three separate classes: the ruling class, virtually immortal thanks to the aliens' biotechnology; the 'betas', genetically human but mentally conditioned to obey the rulers; and the 'azis', a slave class created from normal human stock. Cherryh has also written several fantasy novels, such as *The Dreamstone* (1983), a pseudo-mythological tale set in Dark Age Ireland. Cherryh's first novel, *Gate Of Ivrel* (1976), is an entertaining and convincing story set on a technologically backward world on which political power stems from the super-science of the Gates to other worlds. The hero of the story is Vanye, who, dishonoured and outcast from his clan, becomes involved with Morgaine whose mission it is to destroy the Gates. The tension between Vanye and Morgaine, native and outsider, fleshes out the details of the local culture without breaking the flow of the narrative.

READ•ON
- *Well Of Shiuan* and *Fires Of Azeroth* (sequels to *Gate Of Ivrel*)
  Brothers Of Earth
  Hunter Of Worlds
- ▶ ▷ Ursula K LeGuin, *The Left Hand Of Darkness*
  ▷ Mary Gentle, *Golden Witchbreed*
  Joan Vinge, *The Snow Queen*

CHILDREN AND ADOLESCENTS
▷ Ray Bradbury, *Something Wicked This Way Comes*
▷ John Crowley, *Engine Summer*
▷ Keith Roberts, *Molly Zero*
▷ Gene Wolfe, *The Devil In A Forest*
▷ John Wyndham, *Chocky*
▷ Diana Wynne Jones, *Charmed Life*

CHRISTOPHER, John (born 1922)
British novelist

Christopher's famous *The Death Of Grass* (1956) and *The World In Winter* (1962) are classic post-▷ Wyndham catastrophe novels, showing how fragile our civilisation might be and presenting a vision of the vicious survivalism which might replace it. His world is bleaker than Wyndham's and his heroes are less unshakeably good-natured, but the two writers share a quality of 'Britishness' and a lasting appeal for non-sf readers. Christopher's Tripods trilogy (*The White Mountains, The City Of Gold And Lead* and *The Pool Of Fire*, 1967–8), recently televised by the BBC, is a children's adventure story about a small band of rebels fighting against the giant mechanical tripods – and their surprisingly sympathetic masters – which have enslaved humanity. The way in which the supposedly evil alien invaders are shown to be, personally, quite nice people is remarkably sophisticated, and the books, if less shocking than Christopher's catastrophe novels, are equally disturbing and thought-provoking.

READ•ON
- *The Guardians,* set in a divided future society, shows considerable insight into problems of adolescence and relationships within a framework of children's adventure. *The Prince In Waiting* begins Christopher's other juvenile trilogy.
- ▶ Other uncompromising views of civilisation after a catastrophe:
  ▷ Algis Budrys, *Some Will Not Die*

▷ Keith Roberts, *The Furies*
▷ David Brin, *The Postman*
William Golding, *Lord Of The Flies* describes
a microcosmic society of children,
shipwrecked on an island and reverting to
savagery
▶ To the Tripods trilogy:
Peter Dickinson, *The Changes*
Joan Aiken, *The Wolves Of Willoughby Chase*

CLARKE, Arthur C(harles) (born 1917)
British writer of novels, short stories and non-fiction

Almost all Clarke's work is concerned with the impact of scientific and technological advances on human society or with the implications of contact (or lack of contact) with alien intelligences. His stories show a consistent talent for the presentation of interesting scientific novelties, as well as a gradual improvement in his initially awkward characterisation and prose style. Examples of his early work are *The Sands Of Mars* (1951) and *The Deep Range* (1957), which deals with near-future whale farming. The 2001 series (*2001: A Space Odyssey,* 1968, *2010: Odyssey Two,* 1982, and *2061: Odyssey Three,* 1988) is characteristic of Clarke's maturity, telling the story of humanity's discovery of alien artefacts in the Solar System and the revelations brought by their attempts to make contact. These books contain a good deal of speculation about future space travel and artificial intelligences, and their theme of transcendental evolution due to alien intervention is also the central concern of *Childhood's End* (1953).

RENDEZVOUS WITH RAMA (1973)
This novel is the story of the discovery and exploration of Rama, an initially lifeless spaceship-world which enters the Solar System. As Rama approaches the sun, it starts to wake up, providing surprise after surprise for the crew of the spacecraft sent to investigate it. Most of Clarke's themes are here; the scientific basis of the various discoveries and speculations are lucidly explained without dulling their excitement, though, as in *2001* and *Childhood's End,* mysteries always remain, and Clarke's excitement with the idea of contacting alien intelligences is vividly conveyed.

Clarke's other works include A Fall Of Moondust *(the story of a stranded 'dustcruiser' on the moon, rich in scientific detail),* Imperial Earth *(a well-characterised novel of future political intrigue),* Earthlight, *and the short story collections* The Sentinel *and* The Best of Arthur C Clarke *(including pithy expositions of clever scientific ideas, as well as stories such as 'The Star', in which the Star of Bethlehem is discovered to have been a genocidal nova).*

READ·ON

● *The City And The Stars* describes a pair of complementary pastoral and technological utopias; the explanation of the galactic history that underlies their existence conveys a sense of irrevocable loss. *The Fountains Of Paradise* is a* realistic depiction of the construction of a 'tower' from Earth's surface to geosynchronous orbit, combined with an interesting story of alien contact. *The Exploration Of Space* (non-fiction).

▶ To Clarke's fiction of scientific ideas:
▷ Greg Bear, *Blood Music*
▷ Charles Sheffield, *Between The Strokes Of Night*
▷ Robert Forward, *The Flight Of The Dragon-fly*
▷ Kim Stanley Robinson, *The Memory Of Whiteness*

▶ To Clarke's ideas on first contact:
▷ Richard Cowper, *The Twilight Of Briareus*

▶ To the interest in societies:
▷ Larry Niven, *A Gift From Earth*
▷ John Varley, *The Ophiuchi Hotline*
▷ Bruce Sterling, *Schismatrix*

CLEMENT, Hal (born 1922)
US writer of short stories, novels and non-fiction

Clement is one of the purest of all hard sf writers, his stories being intriguing intellectual games played with the consequences of some scientific supposition. Most of his novels are explorations of strange alien worlds, such as *Close to Critical* (1964, about a planet where the ammonia seas readily turn to vapour, causing 400-foot tides) or the excellent *Mission of Gravity* (1954), set on the bizarre, discus-shaped world of Mesklin, where gravity varies from 3g (at the equator) to 700g (at the poles).

READ·ON

● *The Best Of Hal Clement* (collection) *Needle* is an early sf detective novel, while *Iceworld* and *Cycle Of Fire* involve ingeniously detailed alien biologies.

▶ ▷ Robert L Forward, *Dragon's Egg*
▷ Arthur C Clarke, *A Fall Of Moondust*

COMPTON, D(avid) G(uy) (born 1930)
British novelist

'We're civilised people. We know which implications to ignore.' Compton's prime concern is with the human effects of scientific progress, expressed through moving stories of ordinary people caught up by the misuse or over enthusiastic advance of technology. In *The Continuous Katherine Mortenhoe* (1974) the terminally ill heroine is pursued by a (later repentant) reporter with hidden cameras in his eyes, so that her dying weeks may be made into television entertainment. In *The Electric Crocodile* (1970) artificial intelligence is the vehicle for Compton's investigation of scientific ethics, while *Synthajoy* (1968) describes the commercial and medical abuse of a system for recording and ultimately creating direct experience.

R E A D • O N
- ● *The Silent Multitude*
- ▶ ▷ Bob Shaw, *Other Days, Other Eyes*
- Edgar Pangborn, *A Mirror For Observers*

COMPUTERS AND ARTIFICIAL INTELLIGENCE
- ▷ Gregory Benford, *Across The Sea Of Suns*
- ▷ D G Compton, *The Electric Crocodile*
- David Gerrold, *When Harlie Was One*
- ▷ William Gibson, *Neuromancer*
- ▷ Frank Herbert, *Destination: Void*
- ▷ R A Lafferty, *Arrive At Easterwine*
- Sheila MacLeod, *Xanthe And The Robots*
- ▷ John Sladek, *Roderick*

COOPER, Edmund (born 1926)
British novelist and short story writer

Although novels like *Who Needs Men?* (1972) display a regrettable sexism, most of Cooper's work is entertaining and thought provoking. It frequently involves the disastrous breakdown of society, either directly (as in *Kronk*, 1970) or as background to the story: in *The Last Continent* (1970), black Martian colonists return to an Earth devastated by racial warfare and inhabited by white savages, and *The Cloud Walker* (1973) describes the redevelopment of flight in a Luddite society formed after two nuclear holocausts.

R E A D • O N

● *The Overman Culture* (a growing boy gradually realises that his world has been designed to temper him)
Transit

John CROWLEY • *Little, Big*

Gabriel García MARQUEZ
**ONE HUNDRED YEARS OF
SOLITUDE**
*(an isolated family community as a
microcosm of South American life)*

Peter CAREY
ILLYWHACKER
*(132-year old Australian conman tells
his story)*

▷ Alan GARNER
THE STONE BOOK QUARTET
*(a family portrait exploring people's sense
of roots – and sense of identity)*

Several Generations

Isabel ALLENDE
THE HOUSE OF THE SPIRITS
*(political and personal evolution in rich
South American family over 100 years)*

▷ Clifford SIMAK
CITY
*(humans, intelligent dogs and robots play
part after part in the slow disappearance of
humankind)*

▷ Iain BANKS
THE BRIDGE
*(socially aware yuppie dreams of vast,
nightmarish bridge)*

▷ Gene WOLFE
THE BOOK OF THE NEW SUN
*(the lines of division between life and
death, the old and the new, the future and
the past . . .)*

▷ Ursula K LEGUIN
THE DISPOSSESSED
*(complementary opposites – and the walls
between them)*

▷ Alan GARNER
RED SHIFT
*(a traumatic love story of the present is
worked out through the past)*

Peter ACKROYD
HAWKSMOOR
*(a demonic architect is commissioned to
rebuild London churches after the Great
Fire; then, three hundred years later, the
murders begin . . .)*

▷ Samuel R DELANY
EMPIRE STAR
*(plot motifs recur in ever-changing forms
and from ever-changing perspectives)*

Anna KAVAN
ICE
*(in a Europe entering a final winter, the
narrator's meetings with a mysterious girl
follow a strangely repetitive pattern)*

▷ Brian ALDISS
REPORT ON PROBABILITY A
*(from alternate dimensions, observers
watch other observers who watch . . .)*

Megan LINDHOLM
WIZARD OF THE PIGEONS
*(community of modern-day wizard-tramps
on the streets of Seattle)*

▷ Clive BARKER
WEAVEWORLD
*(a carpet which contains a whole world
– one which occupies the quiet corners of
our own)*

Paul HAZEL
WINTERKING
*(part 3 of the 'Finnbranch', a retelling of
the 'Kalevala' myth)*

▷ Peter BEAGLE
THE FOLK OF THE AIR
*(mediaeval re-enactment society members
are confronted with genuine reincarnation)*

▷ Diana WYNNE JONES
WILKINS' TOOTH
*(witchcraft and teenage rivalry in a leafy
suburb)*

▷ Fritz LEIBER
CONJURE WIFE
(modern day suburban witchcraft)

▶ ▷ Clifford Simak, *Special Deliverance*
▷ John Wyndham, *The Chrysalids*

COWPER, Richard (born 1926)
British novelist and short story writer

Cowper's books contain a rare elegiac mix of science, literacy and humanity. *The Road To Corlay* (1978), now published with the novella *Piper At The Gates Of Dawn,* is set a thousand years hence in a Britain partially flooded by the rising sea, and deals with the oppression of the 'Kinship' cult founded in *Piper.* In *The Twilight Of Briareus* a nearby star goes supernova, with catastrophic results: touching on themes of feminism, redemption and the experience of the alien, with powerful characters, images and descriptions, this is Cowper's richest novel.

R E A D • O N ▶ ▷ Bob Shaw, *Other Days, Other Eyes*
▷ Christopher Priest, *A Dream Of Wessex*
▷ D G Compton, *Synthajoy*
▷ Orson Scott Card, *Capitol* are in similar mode

CROWLEY, John (born 1942)
US novelist

Crowley's *Aegypt,* with its occult complexities and beautiful pastoral visions, was one of 1987's most enchanting novels. Seeking to describe 'how history hungers for the shape of myth', it lay on the furthest edge of conventional fantasy, while its slogan 'there is more than one history of the world' encapsulated the ambiguities Crowley has explored in his work from the start. His early novels, *The Deep* (1975) and *Beasts* (1976), displayed promise, but this only began to be fulfilled with the detailed and carefully structured *Engine Summer* (1979). In search of his love Once A Day, Rush That Speaks (a fine characterisation of a boy growing to maturity) wanders through a post-apocalypse world in its tranquil 'engine' (Indian) summer. With *Little, Big* (1981) came a staggering metamorphosis. Fairies, wizards and reincarnated villains all join in a dense, close-knit tale of contemporary America. Smokey Barnable marries Alice Drinkwater, and so joins a family with intimate links to Faerie through their dreamlike, possibly infinite house Edgewood. Describing the patterns of the past, the story covers several generations of the family, with everything mirroring everything else. Although the book is initially confusing, the reader's perseverance is repaid: 'the further in you go, the bigger it gets', in Crowley's words. Mannered but moving, always preferring the magical over the mundane, the novel has a ▷ Borgesian attention to detail and is brought to a masterly conclusion.

R E A D • O N ▶ ▷ Alan Garner, *The Stone Book Quartet*
▷ Gene Wolfe, *Peace*
Richard Grant, *Rumours Of Spring*
▶ To *Aegypt*:
▷ M John Harrison, *Viriconium Nights*

D

DAVIDSON, Avram (born 1923)
US novelist and short story writer

Davidson is known primarily for his quirkily entertaining shorter works, including 'Or All The Seas With Oysters' (from the 1962 collection of the same name), which reveals the ghastly truth about the secret life of bicycles and coat-hangers. His novels have received less attention, despite their literary, vivid style; especially worth reading are *The Phoenix And The Mirror* (1969), a medieval fantasy featuring the scholar and sorceror Vergil Magus, and *Masters Of The Maze* (1965), a technological adventure which contrasts with the fantastic elements present in most of his other work.

R E A D • O N ● *The Enquiries Of Doctor Esterhazy* (collection)
▶ To *The Phoenix And The Mirror*:
▷ James Blish, *Doctor Mirabilis*
▶ ▷ Fredric Brown, *Nightmares And Geezenstacks*
▷ R A Lafferty, *Nine Hundred Grandmothers*

DE CAMP, L(yon) Sprague
US novelist and short story writer

Amusing adventures set in exotic locales were de Camp's forte. Among the best are the 'Viagens Interplanetarias' sf stories (including the romance *The Search for Zei*, 1962, the collection *The Continent Makers*, 1953, and the serious novel of hive-minds *Rogue Queen*, 1951). De Camp also wrote entertaining fantasies, including the collection *The Tritonian Ring* (1953), set in the time of Atlantis, and the Harold Shea stories, written in collaboration with Fletcher Pratt. Now published as *The Intrepid Enchanter* (1988), these describe the adventures of two psychologists who use symbolic logic as magic to transport themselves to universes of myth and legend.

R E A D • O N   ●   *Lest Darkness Fall* (time travel to ancient Rome)
        The Goblin Tower (man picked to be king for five years before being sacrificed)
▶ ▷ Fritz Leiber, *Swords Against Wizardry*
   ▷ Jack Vance, *City Of The Chasch*

DELANY, Samuel R(ay) (born 1942)
US novelist, short story writer and critic

Delany's writing divides into two main portions. His early works are space operas of steadily increasing sophistication, distinguished by their allusive structure and emphasis on mythic themes. *Nova* (1968) shows these elements strongly, as well as a characteristic concern with the heroic quest and the figure of the young artist/criminal. Explicit myth-references and resonances with the Tarot lend depth to *Nova*'s story of the galaxy-spanning conflict between Lorq Von Ray and the Reds, for a prize wrenched from the heart of an exploding nova. From the same period, the novella 'The Star Pit' (included in *Driftglass*, 1971) examines the responses shown by intelligent beings forced to accept imprisonment by their own limitations. Delany's later books are considerably slower paced, carried along by the momentum of their examinations of social and feminist issues rather than by a dynamic plot. The books' triumph is that the oddities of their people and of their societies reflect upon each other so as to bring out unsuspected truths about both. *Triton: An Ambiguous Heterotopia* (1976) is set in a form of utopia, where personal freedom of choice has become almost overwhelming – entirely so for the male central character, whose rejection of his society reflects intriguingly on our own perceptions of gender roles. *Dhalgren* (1975) is the story of an amnesiac youth's search for identity in a mysterious city whose landscape symbolizes American youth culture.

STARS IN MY POCKET LIKE GRAINS OF SAND (1986)

In this novel, the first half of a diptych, Delany combines almost all of the strengths of his earlier phases. The story, almost all occurring within a single day, describes how the protagonist finds his perfect lover – a tall, acne-scarred homosexual who bites his nails – and then loses him again. The galactic background is both complex and superbly evoked, while the story is told in a prose style that leaps from casual slang to rich poetry. Delany's interests in gender differences and the diversity of cultural ethics find their greatest expression in this novel, partly through his inventive use of language to confuse our expectations and show us our hidden prejudices.

Delany's other works include Babel-17 *and* Empire Star, *an amusing story of interstellar adventure told simultaneously from a multiplicity of different view-*

*points, which first describes and then tries to induce in the reader the ability to
perceive all these viewpoints at once.*

READ·ON

● *The Einstein Intersection* (a densely structured
story of alien colonists on Earth, who must
re-enact the myths of vanished humanity, in
altered form, in order to adapt to their new
home)

Tales Of Nevèrÿon (the first part of the excellent Nevèrÿon series, which approaches such
modern issues as homosexuality from the
viewpoint of fantasy)

▶ To *Nova*:
▷ William Gibson, *Neuromancer*
▷ Alfred Bester, *Tiger! Tiger!*

▶ To *Stars In My Pocket Like Grains Of Sand*:
▷ Frank Herbert, *Dune* shows a similar dense
background

▶ To the mythic themes:
▷ Roger Zelazny, *Lord Of Light*

▶ To Delany's attitudes to sex and gender:
▷ John Varley, *In The Hall Of The Martian Kings*
▷ Theodore Sturgeon, *Venus Plus X*

DETECTIVES AND DETECTION
▷ Isaac Asimov, *The Naked Sun*
▷ Alfred Bester, *The Demolished Man*
▷ Hal Clement, *Needle*
Neil Ferguson, *Putting Out*
Randall Garrett, *Too Many Magicians*
▷ Stanislaw Lem, *The Investigation*
▷ Larry Niven, *The Long ARM Of Gil Hamilton*
▷ Fred Saberhagen, *The Holmes-Dracula File*
Vernor Vinge, *Marooned In Real Time*
▷ Gene Wolfe, *Free Live Free*

DICK, Philip K(endred) (1928–1982)
US novelist and short story writer

The author of more than thirty science fiction novels, almost every one of
which has lasting value, Dick was a poet of insanity and uncertainty, preoc-
cupied with human perceptions and the often blurred distinction between
reality and fantasy. His stories are full of sudden and disorienting alterations

Philip K DICK ● *The Man In The High Castle*

Len DEIGHTON
SS-GB
(thriller set in post-war Britain where the Germans won)

▷ Harry HARRISON
A TRANSATLANTIC TUNNEL, HURRAH!
(Victorian engineers try to link Britain to her American colonies)

▷ Keith ROBERTS
PAVANE
(an England where the Armada won and the Catholic church dominates society)

Alternate Histories

SAKI
WHEN WILLIAM CAME
(London socialites come to terms with German victory in World War I)

Joan AIKEN
THE WOLVES OF WILLOUGHBY CHASE
(political adventure after successful Jacobite rebellion)

▷ Norman SPINRAD
BUG JACK BARRON
(corruption in high places after discovery of longevity treatment draws in populist broadcaster)

▷ Doris LESSING
THE SENTIMENTAL AGENTS IN THE VOLYEN EMPIRE
(shifting power relationships in a three-world system manipulated by outside agents)

Political Intrigue

▷ Isaac ASIMOV
FOUNDATION
(the tiny Foundation survives by manipulation of its more powerful neighbour worlds)

▷ Poul ANDERSON
MIRKHEIM
*(in a decaying galactic civilisation,
powerful factions struggle over the only
source of an immensely valuable element)*

▷ Ursula K LEGUIN:
THE LATHE OF HEAVEN
*(a man whose dreams can alter reality
learns to accept his power through Taoism)*

▷ Robert SHECKLEY
OPTIONS
*(interstellar postman trapped on a world
which defies understanding)*

Taoism

▷ Gregory BENFORD
THE STARS IN SHROUD
*(starship crews remain in tune with each
other by playing a mystical game)*

▷ Hermann HESSE
STEPPENWOLF
*(a deeply divided man searches for
personal transcendence)*

▷ Norman SPINRAD
SONGS FROM THE STARS
*('evil' technology returns to trouble post-
holocaust society's peaceful Way of living)*

of place and personality, told with a bizarre sense of humour and often seen through the eyes of paranoid or schizophrenic characters – as in *Time Out Of Joint* (1959), whose protagonist battles with insanity (or is it?) as he attempts to escape from an entirely spurious world that has been constructed solely for him. Much of Dick's work features people who turn out to be androids or robots, examples including *Do Androids Dream Of Electric Sheep?* (1968), a novel which also demonstrates Dick's preoccupation with entropic decay, and the early short story 'Second Variety', in which humanity itself is replaced by war robots (in *The Variable Man*, 1953). Dick's early novels frequently employ drugs as a means of altering reality, the classic example being *The Three Stigmata Of Palmer Eldritch* (1964), where the characters lose all ability to distinguish true worlds from false; in such later books as *A Scanner Darkly* (1977), however, they are viewed in a profoundly negative fashion. As Dick neared the end of his life, he turned increasingly towards the religious themes anticipated in the messiah figures of such novels as *The World Jones Made* (1956), particularly in the fascinating *Valis* (1981), in which an ancient extraterrestrial satellite beams messages directly into the hero's brain to announce the second coming of the Saviour. His best-known book, *The Man In The High Castle* (1962), involves Eastern religion, altered reality and fascism in a novel in which the Axis forces have won the Second World War and Japan occupies America – and yet their world is somehow not the 'real' one.

A MAZE OF DEATH (1970)

In this novel, an extraordinarily rich combination of such favourite themes as religion, reality and madness, fourteen colonists, each mildly deranged, are sent to the planet of Delmak-O. Surviving with the aid of their scientifically proven religion, they attempt to discover who sent them there and why, but each individual slowly drifts into insanity under the watchful presence of the Building and its mobile cameras. As the planet begins to appear increasingly malevolent and the colonists die one by one, the twists in the plot come ever more frequently, culminating in a startling ending only Dick could have written.

Dick's other novels include The Penultimate Truth, *a post-holocaust novel with a difference,* Eye In The Sky, *an ironic and disturbing insight into a group of people and their private worlds,* Flow My Tears, The Policeman Said, Ubik, Clans Of The Alphane Moon, The Simulacra *and* Radio Free Albemuth, *which reintroduces the satellite from Valis in its description of an extraterrestrially inspired conspiracy in an alternate America where an analogue of Richard Nixon has become the personification of evil.*

READ·ON ● *Martian Time-Slip* (a complex study of schizophrenia)

The Transmigration Of Timothy Archer (a thoughtful study of a religious man in turmoil)
► ▷ Franz Kafka, The Trial
▷ Gene Wolfe, The Fifth Head Of Cerberus
Hunter S Thompson, Fear And Loathing In Las Vegas
▷ K W Jeter, The Glass Hammer
Keri Hulme, The Bone People
▷ William Burroughs, The Naked Lunch
John Fowles, The Magus
Paul Auster, The New York Trilogy
► To the concern with reality:
▷ Brian Aldiss, Report On Probability A
▷ Norman Spinrad, No Direction Home
▷ Josephine Saxton, Queen Of The States

DICKSON, Gordon R(upert) (born 1923)
US novelist and short story writer

Dickson's novels usually take the form of entertaining adventures with deeper implications. Many deal in one way or another with reactions to alien contact, from the pacifism of *Naked to the Stars* (1961) to the colonial warfare of *The Outposter* (1972). The Childe Cycle, which is planned to take up at least twelve volumes, is undoubtedly Dickson's major work. In the series Dickson argues that around the time of the Renaissance humanity began evolving into a different species, a process which will be completed hundreds of years in our future. To date, published novels are *Necromancer* (1962), *Tactics of Mistake* (1971), *Soldier, Ask Not* (1967) (the short version of which won a Hugo), *Dorsai!* (1976) and *The Final Encyclopedia* (1985); and other books are planned, set in the present and past as well as the future. The books describe the splitting of humanity into many highly differentiatied sub-groups, from the philosophical Exotics to the religious Friendlies, each of which expresses a component of our race's essential nature and which begin to breed back with each other to produce a 'New Man'. The series focuses on the Dorsai, extremely strong and skilled mercenaries who represent the militaristic aspect of humanity. (*Tactics Of Mistake,* for example, the first Dorsai book chronologically, is about how the innovative strategist Cletus Grahame battles to win the colonies freedom from Earth's influence.)

READ·ON
● *Lost Dorsai* and *The Spirit Of Dorsai* are non-Cycle Dorsai books, while *Time Storm* and *Home From The Shore* are non-series
► To the warrior Dorsai:

▷ Jerry Pournelle, *Future History*
► To the evolutionary mysticism:
▷ Frank Herbert, the *Dune* books

DISCH, Thomas M(ichael) (born 1940)
US novelist, short story writer and poet

Deep pessimism is the hallmark of Disch's writing, along with a gift for creating very human characters. His feeling for black comedy and fascination with the nature of the artist are often apparent in his stories, but Disch has too many talents to be pinned down by simple definitions. His short fiction (the best of which is collected in *Under Compulsion,* 1968 and *Getting Into Death,* 1976) varies from surreal fables of dislocation to minutely observed tales of the near future. Among his sf novels are *Camp Concentration* (1968), the vividly presented story of a military experiment which increases the intelligence of its unwilling subjects and then kills them, and *On Wings Of Song* (1979), an analysis in sf images of freedom and responsibility. *334* (1972) is a collection of linked stories set in a future Manhattan. They examine such themes as the weariness brought by experience, the victory of entropy and the fragility of youth, through the characters of the people who inhabit the (powerfully described) apartment block number 334.

READ·ON

● *The Genocides* (set on an Earth conquered by aliens chillingly indifferent to humanity)
Here I Am, There You Are, Where Were We? (poetry)
Amnesia (an interactive 'novel' that can be 'played' on a computer)
The Businessman (nightmarishly comic religious fantasy)
► To the short stories:
Garry Kilworth, *The Songbirds Of Pain*
Chris Burns, *About The Body*
► To *Camp Concentration*:
Thomas Mann, *Doctor Faustus*
► To *334*:
▷ M John Harrison, *Viriconium Nights*

DONALDSON, Stephen (born 1947)
US novelist and short story writer

Donaldson's reputation, as one of the most successful fantasy writers since ▷ Tolkien, rests on two blockbusting series. His novels reflect at length on themes of guilt and redemption, alienation and obsession, power and dependence; his protagonists have the potential to be the saviours of those around them, but find that even when they rely emotionally on people, they are unable to help them. *The Mirror Of Her Dreams* (1986) and *A Man Rides Through* (1988) tell the tale of Terisa Morgan, transplanted from a New York condominium to the threatened fantasy land of Mordant. The novels' complicated and intriguing plot compensates for the rather vague background, and Terisa's desperate loneliness is effectively portrayed. The first book ends on a cliff-hanger, so that it is impossible to read it in isolation. (The series interestingly mirrors *The Chronicles Of Thomas Covenant* (see below), in which background predominates over plot and the protagonist is far more active and aggressive.)

THE CHRONICLES OF THOMAS COVENANT (1977–83)

A vivid and colourful background, a powerfully characterised hero (or anti-hero), a plot drawing on the messianic myth, a succession of strong set pieces and a wildly metaphorical writing style all combine in this 6-novel series to produce one of the most striking fantasies of the post-Tolkien era. The first trilogy (*Lord Foul's Bane*, *The Illearth War* and *The Power That Preserves*) sees leprosy victim Thomas Covenant summoned to the pastoral utopia of the Land, which is under threat from Lord Foul the Destroyer. Covenant's white gold wedding ring is a talisman of power, but he is paralysed by his refusal to accept this new world, because he fears it is a delusion arising from his illness. His attempts to reconcile his disease with the purity he sees in the Land, and his struggle to understand whether his experiences are anything more than an externalisation of his own mental agonies, provide a focal point for the story. In the second trilogy (*The Wounded Land*, *The One Tree* and *White Gold Wielder*), Covenant returns to the Land 4000 years – only ten of his – later. By this time Lord Foul has corrupted even the sun to his ends and needs only Covenant's white gold to achieve his ultimate aims. This time accepting his responsibility, Covenant undertakes a quest to defeat Foul – but his power is dangerously uncontrolled, and to use it risks destruction. Although many find Donaldson's writing style increasingly impenetrable here, the reader's perseverance is rewarded by richer characterisation and background than in the first trilogy, a broadening of themes, and a powerful climax.

Donaldson's other books are Daughter Of Regals, *a collection which shows him in less weighty mood, and* Gilden-Fire, *a short 'out-take' from* The Illearth War.

READ·ON ▶ To the plotting and politicking of *The Mirror Of Her Dreams*:
  ▷ Guy Gavriel Kay, *The Summer Tree*
  ▷ Roger Zelazny, *Nine Princes In Amber*
  ▶ To the second Covenant trilogy:
  ▷ Gene Wolfe, *The Book Of The New Sun*

Stephen DONALDSON
The First Chronicles Of Thomas Covenant

▷ Michael MOORCOCK
STORMBRINGER
(Prince Elric destroys his people, kills his wives and betrays his gods)

Lynn ABBEY
DAUGHTER OF THE BRIGHT FLAME
(Rifkind, healer and warrior, sets out on a quest for her destiny after her clan is massacred)

The Alienated Hero

▷ M John HARRISON
IN VIRICONIUM
(Ashlyme tries to persuade his decadent friends to act to save a brilliant painter)

▷ Fredric BROWN
WHAT MAD UNIVERSE
(magazine editor finds himself in a baffling sf world – and is lucky to survive)

▷ Andre NORTON
WITCH WORLD
(an ex-soldier in a world where witches fight extradimensional technological invaders)

Unexpectedly Transplanted From Own World

▷ Philip José FARMER
MAKER OF UNIVERSES
(rejuvenated academic finds himself very much at home in bizarre custom-designed worlds)

▷ J R R TOLKIEN
THE LORD OF THE RINGS
(a shadow from the past threatens Middle-Earth – unless a small Fellowship can strike at the heart of his power)

Patricia WREDE
THE SEVEN TOWERS
(the seven kingdoms threatened by the return of the Red Plague)

Personifications Of Ultimate Evil

▷ Tim POWERS
DINNER AT DEVIANT'S PALACE
*(charismatic leader of Moonie-like cult
turns out to have a certain taste for souls)*

▷ Clive BARKER
WEAVEWORLD
*(the Fugue is threatened by the Salesman,
who promises to grant your deepest wish,
the Incantatrix Immacolata and her two
sisters, and the angelic-demonic Scourge)*

▷ Guy Gavriel KAY
THE SUMMER TREE
*(the imprisoned god Rakoth Maugrim
is free again, and Fionavar faces
destruction)*

Megan LINDHOLM
WIZARD OF THE PIGEONS
*(Vietnam veteran, now street wizard, is
haunted by the ultimate evil: his past)*

▷ Robert SHECKLEY
OPTIONS
*(Harmonia: childish game, fragmented
hallucination or insane reality?)*

▷ Philip K DICK
**THE THREE STIGMATA OF
PALMER ELDRITCH**
*(Martian colonists relieve their boredom
with drugs which ultimately become
stronger than reality)*

Internal Or External?

▷ Gene WOLFE
PEACE
*(Alden Dennis Weer drifts through an
ambiguous, shifting past)*

▷ Ursula K LEGUIN
THE LATHE OF HEAVEN
(a man's dreams alter the world)

▷ Josephine SAXTON
QUEEN OF THE STATES
*(Magdalen Hayward's deranged fantasies
are projected onto the lives of those who
live around her)*

> ▶ Other intellectually appealing fantasy adventures include:
> Paul Hazel, *The Finnbranch*
> ▷ Geoff Ryman, *The Warrior Who Carried Life*
> Megan Lindholm, *Wizard Of The Pigeons*
> Rachel Pollack, *Unquenchable Fire*
> ▷ Clive Barker, *Weaveworld*

DRUGS
> ▷ Brian Aldiss, *Barefoot In The Head*
> ▷ William Burroughs, *The Naked Lunch*
> Hunt Collins, *Tomorrow And Tomorrow*
> ▷ Philip K Dick, *A Scanner Darkly*
> Robert Shea and ▷ Robert Anton Wilson, *Illuminatus!*
> ▷ Robert Silverberg, *A Time Of Changes*

DUNSANY, Lord (1878–1957)
British writer of short stories, novels, poems, plays and essays

Dunsany wrote short tales of fantasy laid in imaginary countries of his own invention 'at the edge of the world'. Such pieces as 'Carcassonne' (the story of a band of knights who challenge Fate itself in their search for a lost city, in *At The Edge Of The World,* 1970) are witty, stylish and endlessly inventive, easily the equal of any more modern fantasy.

READ·ON
> ● *Beyond The Fields We Know* (collection)
> *The King Of Elfland's Daughter* is an excellent fantasy novel
> ▶ ▷ James Branch Cabell, *Figures Of Earth*
> ▷ E R Eddison, *The Worm Ouroboros*

E

EASTERN EUROPEAN SF
> C G Bearne ed, *Vortex*
> ▷ Karel Čapek, *War With The Newts*
> ▷ Stanislaw Lem, *Solaris*
> Josef Nesvadba, *In The Footsteps Of The Abominable Snowman*

▷ Arkady and Boris Strugatsky, *The Snail On The Slope*
Vladimir Voinovich, *Moscow 2042*
Ivan Yefremov, *Andromeda*
▷ Yevgeny Zamyatin, *We*

ECOLOGY

▷ Brian Aldiss, *Helliconia Spring*
▷ Piers Anthony, *Omnivore*
▷ Gregory Benford, *Across The Sea Of Suns*
▷ John Brunner, *The Sheep Look Up*
▷ Frank Herbert, *Dune*
▷ George R R Martin, *Tuf Voyaging*
Alan Moore with Steve Bissette and John Totleben, *The Saga Of The Swamp Thing Part I* (graphic novel)
▷ Brian Stableford, *Critical Threshold*
Philip Wylie, *The End Of The Dream*

EDDINGS, David (born 1931)
US novelist

Eddings's fantasy is typical of the post-▷ Tolkien school. It consists of two closely related series of five books each, the Belgariad and the Malloreon (only three books of the latter have as yet been published). Instead of relying on a detailed background, as Tolkien's fictions do, these books are marked by a strong sense of irony, with humorous interludes breaking up the plot. The first book of the Belgariad is *Pawn of Prophecy* (1983). Garion, a young farm lad, discovers that his ordinary-seeming aunt is in fact a powerful sorceress, and slowly realises that he too has the ability to become a wizard. He is not destined for a peaceful life; dark prophecy is moving against light prophecy, and he is just a pawn in their battle. The twin themes of destiny and prophecy are often mentioned in the Belgariad, especially in its first book, and much that occurs is predicted by the various prophecies, which are intelligent beings seemingly in control of events. Another feature is the unusual magic system, incorporating Newton's law that for every action there is an equal and opposite reaction, so that a magician trying to lift a five ton rock has to cope with five tons of pressure on his brain.

READ·ON

● *Queen Of Sorcery.* The first book of the Malloreon is *Guardians Of The West*
▶ ▷ Piers Anthony, *A Spell for Chameleon*
▷ Alan Dean Foster, *Spellsinger*
▷ Jack Vance's *Lyonesse* is denser and more literary, but no less engrossing

EDDISON, E(ric) R(ucker) (1882–1945)
British novelist

Eddison is one of the most difficult and yet rewarding of early fantasy novelists. The Zimiamvian trilogy (*Mistress Of Mistresses, A Fish Dinner In Memison* and *The Mezentian Gate,* 1935–41) is set both in the modern world and in the ideal world Zimiamvia, which is nevertheless not a utopia; the beauty and atmosphere of Zimiamvia are excellently conveyed by Eddison's skilful use of archaic English. *Mistress Of Mistresses,* in particular, is a brilliant novel of politics and intrigue, with underlying themes of love and divinity.

READ·ON
- ● *The Worm Ourobouros*
- ▶ *Laxdaela Saga* (Penguin translation)
- ▷ Lord Dunsany, *The King Of Elfland's Daughter*
- ▷ Mervyn Peake, *Titus Groan*
-    William Morris, *The Well At The World's End*

THE EDGE OF SF
(books which push at the boundaries of sf)
- ▷ Jorge Luis Borges, *Labyrinths*
-    Italo Calvino, *Cosmicomics*
- ▷ John Crowley, *Aegypt*
-    Keri Hulme, *The Windeater/Te Kaihau*
-    Anna Kavan, *Ice*
-    Alberto Manguel ed, *Black Water*
-    Gabriel Garcia Marquez, *100 Years Of Solitude*
- ▷ Thomas Pynchon, *Gravity's Rainbow*
-    Salman Rushdie, *Midnight's Children*
- ▷ Gene Wolfe, *Peace*

ELLISON, Harlan (born 1934)
US novelist, short story writer, essayist and editor

Passionate concern for moral questions has always inspired Ellison's work, though the other side of this strength is his tendency to over-emphasis (particularly evident in his very early work of the 1950s). Nevertheless, his commitment to such themes as hypocrisy, the value of the individual and the nature of evil has produced such superb and highly readable stories as 'Repent, Harlequin, Said The Ticktockman!', a savage parable about authoritarianism, and 'The Whimper Of Whipped Dogs', which describes a timid woman's gradual possession by the spirit of violence and hatred which animates the modern city. The best of these pieces are included in the collection of 'modern myths' *Deathbird Stories* (1975) and *The Essential Ellison*

(1987), which also contains such experimental stories as 'The Beast That Shouted Love At The Heart Of The World' (a circularly written description of eternal psychosis). *Shatterday* (1982), Ellison's most recent original collection, includes the moving study of nostalgia 'Jeffty Is Five'.

READ·ON

● *Web Of The City* (a non-sf novel based on the time Ellison spent under a false identity running with a Brooklyn street gang)
Love Ain't Nothing But Sex Misspelled (collection)
The Glass Teat (essays)
Dangerous Visions (edited by Ellison; one of the seminal anthologies of the American New Wave)

▶ ▷ William Burroughs, *Nova Express*
▷ Lucius Shepard, *The Jaguar Hunter*

EXPERIMENTAL WRITING

▷ Brian Aldiss, *Barefoot In The Head*
▷ J G Ballard, *The Atrocity Exhibition*
▷ William S Burroughs, *The Naked Lunch*
Langdon Jones ed, *The New SF*
▷ Michael Moorcock, *The Condition Of Muzak*
▷ Robert Sheckley, *Options*
D M Thomas, *Ararat*

F

FANTASY EMPIRES

Glen Cook, *All Darkness Met*
▷ E R Eddison, *Mistress Of Mistresses*
▷ Tanith Lee, *The Storm Lord*
▷ Julian May, *The Nonborn King*
▷ Michael Moorcock, *The History Of The Runestaff*
▷ J R R Tolkien, *The Lord Of The Rings*
▷ Gene Wolfe, *The Book Of The New Sun*

FANTASY QUESTS

Brian Bates, *The Way Of Wyrd*
Diane Duane, *The Door Into Fire*
Barry Hughart, *Bridge Of Birds*
▷ Tanith Lee, *The Birthgrave*
▷ Patricia McKillip, *The Riddle-Master Of Hed*
Robin McKinley, *The Blue Sword*
▷ Michael Moorcock, *The Warhound And The World's Pain*
▷ Geoff Ryman, *The Warrior Who Carried Life*
▷ Jack Vance, *Lyonesse*
▷ Roger Zelazny, *Eye Of Cat*

FARMER, Philip José (born 1918)
US novelist and short story writer

One of the few true mould-breakers in sf, Farmer was the first to attempt a serious treatment of sexual love, in *The Lovers* (1961). He has returned to this territory frequently, notably in *Flesh* (1960, depicting a future matriarchy based on the power of sex), and *A Feast Unknown* (1969, in which Tarzan and Doc Savage duel with their immense erect penises). Farmer often uses existing fictional characters to investigate the process of popular myth- or hero-making in such works as *Tarzan Alive* (1972) and *The Other Log Of Phileas Fogg* (1973); he has also written much work by 'fictional authors', including ▷ Vonnegut's Kilgore Trout (*Venus On The Half-Shell*, 1975). His short fiction is noted for experimentation: a good collection is *The Book Of Philip José Farmer*, which includes the Hugo-winning 'Riders Of The Purple Wage', a dazzling description of an artist's life in a future utopia. In *To Your Scattered Bodies Go* (1971) all of humanity has been resurrected along the banks of a huge river by an unknown agency. Among the protagonists are Richard Burton, the explorer, Alice Hargreaves of Wonderland fame, and the sf writer 'Peter Jairus Frigate'. The novel and its sequels *The Fabulous Riverboat, The Dark Design* and *The Magic Labyrinth* (1971–80) examine religious belief, power in interpersonal relationships, and the possibility of absolute morality through the characters' search for the identity and purpose of their mysterious benefactors.

READ·ON

● *Night Of Light* (a powerful study of religious experience)
Maker Of Universes, and sequels (entertaining adventures set in bizarre linked mini-worlds)
▶ To the stories:
▷ William Burroughs, *The Soft Machine*
▶ Richard Lupoff, *Circumpolar!*

> ▷ Norman Spinrad, *Child Of Fortune*
> Jody Scott, *Passing For Human*

FEIST, Raymond Elias
US novelist

Formerly a designer of role-playing games, Feist has brought a craftsman's sense of detail to the construction of his fantasy novels. These are traditional in form, and are told with verve and swagger. They include *Magician, Silverthorn* and *A Darkness At Sethanon* (collectively *The Riftwar Saga,* 1983–86), and the related *Daughter Of The Empire* (1987).

READ·ON ▶   Michael Scott Rohan, *The Anvil Of Ice*
                    ▷ Michael Moorcock, *The Knight Of The Swords*

FEMINISM
- ▷ Margaret Atwood, *The Handmaid's Tale*
- ▷ Marion Zimmer Bradley, *The Shattered Chain*
- ▷ Angela Carter, *The Passion Of New Eve*
-   Suzy McKee Charnas, *Motherlines*
- ▷ Samuel Delany, *Triton*
-   Suzette Haden Elgin, *Native Tongue*
-   Jen Green and Sarah LeFanu ed, *Despatches From The Frontiers Of The Female Mind*
- ▷ Ursula K LeGuin, *The Left Hand Of Darkness*
- ▷ Marge Piercy, *Woman On The Edge Of Time*
- ▷ Joanna Russ, *The Female Man*

FIRST CONTACT
- ▷ Orson Scott Card, *Speaker For The Dead*
- ▷ Arthur C Clarke, *2001*
-   James Gunn, *The Listeners*
- ▷ Joe Haldeman, *Mindbridge*
- ▷ Stanislaw Lem, *Solaris*
- ▷ Larry Niven and ▷ Jerry Pournelle, *The Mote In God's Eye*
-   Walter Tevis, *The Man Who Fell To Earth*

FORWARD, Robert L (born 1932)
US novelist

Forward has a background in astrophysics, and his novels are impressive examples of scientifically oriented sf – full of imaginative and credible developments of physics. *Dragon's Egg* (1980) describes an expedition which discovers a civilisation on the surface of a neutron star, made up of tiny beings who live much faster than humans. In the sequel, *Starquake* (1988), a tremor on the star's surface destroys the alien society. *The Flight of the Dragonfly* (1984) deals with an interstellar probe, driven by star winds, which discovers a double planet system whose oceans sometimes intermingle.

R E A D • O N   ▶ ▷ Greg Bear, *Eon*
　　　　　　　　　　 ▷ Arthur C Clarke, *Rendezvous with Rama*
　　　　　　　　　　　 Paul Preuss, *Broken Symmetries*

FOSTER, Alan Dean (born 1946)
US novelist

In his early career Foster was known for such sf work as *Midworld, Icerigger* and *The Tar-Aiym Krang*. These strongly plotted novels show a well-developed sense of drama and wonder, elements which have been taken further in his more recent fantasy work. The six Spellsinger novels, set in a world of human-sized talking animals, are notable for their freshness and invention. Foster regularly writes novelisations of film scripts, including *Dark Star, Alien/s, Outland* and the *Star Trek Logs* (from the cartoon series).

R E A D • O N   ▶ ▷ Piers Anthony, *A Spell For Chameleon*
　　　　　　　　　　 Christopher Stasheff, *The Warlock in Spite of Himself*

FUTURE SOCIETIES
　▷ Ray Bradbury, *Fahrenheit 451*
　▷ John Brunner, *The Jagged Orbit*
　▷ Samuel R Delany, *Stars In My Pocket Like Grains Of Sand*
　▷ Philip K Dick, *Clans Of The Alphane Moon*
　▷ William Gibson, *Mona Lisa Overdrive*
　▷ Aldous Huxley, *Brave New World*
　▷ Gwyneth Jones, *Escape Plans*
　▷ C M Kornbluth, *The Syndic*
　▷ Ursula K LeGuin, *The Dispossessed*
　▷ Robert Silverberg, *The World Inside*

G

GARNER, Alan (born 1934)
British novelist

Such early works as *The Weirdstone Of Brisingamen* (1960) are children's fantasies, showing ▷ Tolkien's influence but rooted not so much in a fantasy world as in the author's native Cheshire. Later books deal with Garner's constant themes (people's sense of place and individual history) in a more adult fashion, through the re-enactment of myth (*The Owl Service,* 1967) or the working out of the violence and tragedy of the distant past in a love story of the present day (*Red Shift,* 1973).

R E A D • O N
- ● *The Stone Book Quartet* (epitomising Garner's themes through a family's relationship with their surroundings)
- ► ▷ Diana Wynne Jones, *Cart And Cwidder*
  Susan Cooper, *Mandrake*
- ► To *The Weirdstone Of Brisingamen*:
  Joy Chant, *Red Moon And Black Mountain*

GENTLE, Mary (born 1956)
British novelist

Golden Witchbreed (1983) is the story of the interaction between a young Earthwoman, Christie, and the natives of the planet Orthe to which she is envoy. Much of the book revolves around Orthe's social and political structures (and their various intrigues), which are worked out in fine detail. The culture of the Ortheans, disarmingly human-like on the surface, has its alienness slowly revealed as Christie discovers unexpected facets of ethics and sexuality. *Ancient Light* (1987) details the conflict between Orthe and an Earth-based 'multicorporate' which wants access to old Orthean technology.

R E A D • O N
- ► ▷ C J Cherryh, *Brothers Of Earth*
  Jane Yolen, *Cards Of Grief*
- ▷ Michael Bishop, *A Funeral For The Eyes Of Fire*

GIBSON, William (born 1948)
US novelist and short story writer

As the world rolls irresistibly on towards the 1990s, running at an ever increas-

William GIBSON • *Neuromancer*

Walter Jon WILLIAMS
HARDWIRED
*(pilots and programmed killers
increasingly integrated with their
machines)*

▷ Bruce STERLING
SCHISMATRIX
*(across the solar system, humanity
splinters into many different forms)*

**Cyberpunk: a modern genre of sf
dealing with sleazy, hi-tech futures**

Michael SWANWICK
VACUUM FLOWERS
*(Rebel Elizabeth Mudlock runs from the
corporation which holds copyright on her
personality)*

Richard KADREY
METROPHAGE
*(the abuses of power and the diseases of the
city in a decayed future L.A.)*

▷ Samuel R DELANY
NOVA
*(a deadly contest for a supply of an almost
priceless element, a strangely matched
starship crew, a Tarot reader and a young
artist . . .)*

▷ Alfred BESTER
**TIGER! TIGER!/THE STARS MY
DESTINATION**
*(Gully Foyle, left to die in a spaceship
wreck, seeks extravagant revenge)*

Tough, Sleazy Underworld

Dashiell HAMMETT
THE GLASS KEY
*(murder, framing and petty Prohibition
politics)*

Raymond CHANDLER
FAREWELL, MY LOVELY
*(tough guy detective sucked into a sordid
story of greed and betrayal)*

▷ John VARLEY
THE OPHIUCHI HOTLINE
(a grand tour through a Solar System

where humans, paired with symbiotic plants, can live naked in open space, and death itself is only temporary)

▷ Samuel R DELANY
STARS IN MY POCKET LIKE GRAINS OF SAND
(only the representatives of the connecting Web can begin to coordinate the gigantic flow of information between them)

▷ Gwyneth JONES
ESCAPE PLANS
(a society where information systems have become as vital and omnipresent as air)

▷ Larry NIVEN
TALES OF KNOWN SPACE
(fascinating idea stories set in a future full of technological marvels)

Vividly **R**ealised, **H**ighly **T**echnological **F**utures

▷ Michael MOORCOCK and Langdon JONES ed
THE NATURE OF THE CATASTROPHE
(a selection of stories about quintessential 1960s hero Jerry Cornelius)

▷ William BURROUGHS
NOVA EXPRESS
(extraterrestrials with apomorphine try to save humanity from drugs)

▷ J G BALLARD
THE ATROCITY EXHIBITION
(a gallery of disjointed, disturbing images – from dead astronauts to Ronald Reagan)

Analysing **M**odern **P**op **C**ultures

▷ Harlan ELLISON
DEATHBIRD STORIES
(myths for our times – from seductive, treacherous slot machines to a beneficent Satan)

Tom WOLFE
THE KANDY-KOLOURED TANGERINE-FLAKE STREAMLINE BABY
(innovative journalism that catches the essences of the splintered sub-cultures of 1960s America)

ing pace towards an unknown destination, a new pop culture is appearing, a synthesis of high-gloss visual style and hard rock sound, tomorrow's technologies and today's cool, casual amorality. This, at any rate, is Gibson's belief. Despite the many readers who think that he writes exciting, inventive sf set among the sleazy criminal elements of future societies, Gibson sees himself as creating a kind of ultimate distillation of the cultural patterns of our time – a claim whose accuracy is perhaps proved by his immense popularity. The short stories in *Burning Chrome* (1986) are typical of his style: fast plotting, intense visual description, detailed projections of such modern technologies as bio-engineering and telecommunications. *Neuromancer* (1984) begins a loosely connected trilogy set in a future epitomised by the Sprawl, a vast urban conurbation whose inhabitants range from the lethal Molly, with her razor-tipped fingers and implanted mirrorshades, to the 'console cowboy' Case who steals corporate data from cyberspace (the global computer network). Despite flat characterisation, *Neuromancer* tells an exciting story of the awakening of a giant artificial intelligence, while the sequels (*Count Zero*, 1986, and *Mona Lisa Overdrive*, 1988) demonstrate considerably improved technique as they show how the fragments of the intelligence become like gods to the users of cyberspace.

READ·ON　　▶ ▷ K W Jeter, *Dr Adder*
　　　　　　　　　▷ John Brunner, *The Shockwave Rider*

H

HALDEMAN, Joe (born 1943)
US novelist and short story writer

Haldeman's work is technologically oriented, featuring plausible and ingenious scientific ideas, and often strongly moral in intent. His style is harsh and sometimes bitter, suiting his competent, aggressive protagonists. *Tool Of The Trade* (1987) is a near future sf/espionage thriller, while *Worlds* (1981) and *Worlds Apart* (1983) – the first two volumes of a projected trilogy – deal respectively with the social breakdown on Earth immediately before a cataclysmic war, and the (later) attempts of Earth's orbiting colonies to rebuild both the ruined Earth and their own damaged environments. *The Forever War* (1975) is a powerfully realistic novel of interstellar war, influenced by Haldeman's own experiences in Vietnam. Particularly well-depicted is the culture shock which the soldiers suffer because of relativistic time dilations that mean centuries may pass between their returns to Earth. *Mindbridge*

(1976), written in a documentary style resembling that of ▷ Brunner's *Stand On Zanzibar,* involves direct narrative, official documents and explanatory sections set far in the future of the story. The early parts describe the technology of matter transmission and its use by specially trained interstellar explorers, focusing on their discovery of an alien animal that allows telepathic communication. Subsequently, the animal is used in attempts to communicate with an alien race who regard humanity as unfit for the stars.

R E A D • O N

- ● *Infinite Dreams* (collection)
  War Year (a non-sf novel about Vietnam) is difficult to get hold of, but worth the effort.
- ▶ To *The Forever War*:
  - ▷ Lucius Shepard, *Life During Wartime*
  - ▷ Robert Heinlein, *Starship Troopers* presents an opposite view of warfare
- ▶ ▷ Larry Niven, *Protector*
  - ▷ John Varley, *The Ophiuchi Hotline*

HAMBLY, Barbara
US novelist

In Hambly's most successful work, the Darwath trilogy (*The Time Of The Dark, The Walls Of Air* and *The Armies Of Daylight,* 1985–86), a mediaeval fantasy world is threatened by the subterranean horror known as the Dark. Hambly's characterisation, especially of females, is impressive, with even minor characters vividly drawn, and her backgrounds and plots are convincing and logical, never relying on gimmickry. Even such apparent oddities as sexual equality in a medieval society are well-explained, and the motivations of the various sides lend an intriguing sting in the tail to the trilogy.

R E A D • O N

- ● *The Ladies Of Mandrigyn*
- ▶ ▷ Ursula K LeGuin, *A Wizard Of Earthsea*
  Graham Dunstan Martin, *The Soul Master*
  Diane Duane, *The Door Into Fire*

HARRISON, Harry (born 1925)
US novelist and short story writer

Harrison's writing has a diversity found in the work of few other sf writers. It ranges from parody (such as the hilarious *Bill, The Galactic Hero,* 1965, about soldiers in a galaxy-spanning genocidal war) through adventure (*Deathworld,* 1960, set on the most dangerous planet known to humanity) to social warning (*Make Room! Make Room!,* 1966; see below) and alternate realities (*A Transatlantic Tunnel, Hurrah!,* 1972, envisages a world where America is a colony of imperial Britain). His Stainless Steel Rat books are an enjoyable mixture of adventure and humour, featuring the partially reformed criminal Slippery Jim diGriz and the lethal Angelina. *Make Room! Make Room!* is a bleak vision of America at the turn of the next century, when 35 million starving people are crammed into the city of New York. Despite this, the population is continually increasing, with those who advocate birth control decried as unnatural baby-killers. Against the brilliantly drawn background of the suffocating city, policeman Andy Rusch and his colleagues struggle to keep order in the face of low morale and a searing heatwave.

READ·ON   ●   *Star Smashers Of The Galaxy Rangers* (an outrageous space opera spoof)
The Technicolor Time Machine (an amusing story of Hollywood's exploitation of time travel
West Of Eden (set on an alternate Earth with an advanced reptilian civilisation)
▶   To *Make Room! Make Room!*:
▷ Frederik Pohl, *The Years Of The City*
▷ John Brunner, *Stand On Zanzibar*
▶   To *Bill, The Galactic Hero*:
▷ Bob Shaw, *Who Goes Here?*
▷ John Sladek, *The Reproductive System*

HARRISON, M(ichael) John (born 1945)
British novelist and short story writer

Harrison's evocative descriptions of people and places gradually running down made him pre-eminent in ▷ Moorcock's *New Worlds* movement. The stories in *The Ice Monkey* (1975) revolve around the theme of entropy, usually running down themselves rather than coming to any spectacular climax. Harrison was also an enthusiastic participant in the Jerry Cornelius project (see Moorcock), and wrote a New Wave space opera, *The Centauri Device*. One of Harrison's earliest creations is Viriconium, first seen in *The Pastel City* (1971), and revisited in *A Storm Of Wings* (1980), the atmospheric story of an ambiguous and partly metaphysical alien invasion. Viriconium is most potently described, as 'the eternal city which is all cities', in the elegiac, moving tale of redemption *In Viriconium* (1982). The Low City is afflicted by a 'plague', which induces in its victims an all-consuming ennui. Ashlyme the painter wishes to rescue the artist Audsley King, but his friends in the decadent High City, more interested in the comical antics of the city's drunken gods, will not take him seriously. The city's paralysis of will echoes Harrison's entropy theme, and though the novel ends with Viriconium saved, a deep sadness and frustration at

Ashlyme's impotence lingers. As with 1985's excellent follow-up collection *Viriconium Nights,* now published with *In Viriconium* as *Viriconium,* the character portraits and the cityscapes are worth the price of admission alone.

READ•ON

● *The Committed Men*
▶ ▷ J G Ballard, *Vermilion Sands*
  Colin Greenland, *Daybreak On A Different Mountain*
  ▷ Christopher Priest, *An Infinite Summer*
  ▷ D G Compton, *The Silent Multitude*
▶ To the Viriconium books:
  ▷ Mervyn Peake, *Titus Groan*
  Ed Bryant, *Cinnabar*
  ▷ Samuel R Delany, *Dhalgren*

HEINLEIN, Robert A(nson) (1907–88)
US novelist and short story writer

Heinlein's main strength lay in his unusual ideas about sex and war, government and religion, many of which commented interestingly on the American society of the time. His backgrounds are ingenious and conveyed with terse economy, while most of his stories are notable for their fast pace and wisecracking style. Nevertheless, his characters (particularly women) suffer from lack of depth, and many readers perceive him as excessively right-wing. In fact his views originate in an unusually strong sense of the value of individual liberty and responsibility. His early output includes many fresh and ingenious short stories, such as 'All You Zombies' (in the 1959 collection *The Menace From Earth*), which plays logic-games with the subject of time travel. In the 1950s Heinlein moved into the production of such immensely popular teenage sf adventure novels as *Citizen Of The Galaxy* (1957), as well as writing *Starship Troopers* (1959), a novel of future interstellar war remarkable for its advocacy of professional soldiering as a moral duty. Most of his novels since 1970, such as *Time Enough For Love* (1973), concentrate to a marked degree on sexual matters (particularly incest) and tend both to a hectoring tone and a noticeable decrease in the flow of original ideas that made their author famous.

STRANGER IN A STRANGE LAND (1961)
The protagonist of this Hugo-winning novel is Valentine Michael Smith, a young man raised by native Martians after the failure of a manned mission to Mars. Returned to Earth by a second expedition, he becomes a protégé of Jubal Harshaw, author, sybarite and one of Heinlein's ubiquitous father-figures. Smith's assimilation into Earth (ie American) culture is

Frank HERBERT • *Dune*

▷ Samuel R DELANY
**STARS IN MY POCKET LIKE
GRAINS OF SAND**
*(in a civilisation so complex that true
empire is impossible, the Web controls the
flow of information)*

▷ Poul ANDERSON
ENSIGN FLANDRY
*(the rotting Terran Empire struggles with
the young and vital Merseians)*

Galactic Empires

▷ Larry NIVEN and ▷ Jerry
POURNELLE
THE MOTE IN GOD'S EYE
*(set in an empire where rebellion is
ruthlessly suppressed to prevent any
possibility of a second genocidal galactic
war)*

▷ Isaac ASIMOV
THE STARS LIKE DUST
*(idealistic hero attempts to throw off vile
yoke – but finds only plots within plots)*

▷ Gordon R DICKSON:
DORSAI!
*(colonists on an infertile, high-gravity
world, the Dorsai become the finest
mercenaries ever known)*

▷ Jerry POURNELLE
FUTURE HISTORY
*(a military genius fights to maintain the
stability of Earth's colony worlds)*

Warriors

▷ Fred SABERHAGEN
BERSERKER'S PLANET
*(tourists on a primitive world become
involved in its savage ritual combats,
exposing the true characters behind the
civilised surfaces)*

▷ Robert A HEINLEIN
STARSHIP TROOPERS
*(set in a future where professional
soldiering is viewed by many as a moral
duty)*

▷ Ursula K LEGUIN
THE WORD FOR WORLD IS FOREST
(literal 'little green men' are ruthlessly exploited for the wood in their forests)

▷ Anne McCAFFREY
DRAGONFLIGHT
(fairly pleasant feudal system on a colony world)

Native Humans

▷ Poul ANDERSON
VIRGIN PLANET
(abandoned colony is found to have become an all-female society)

▷ Robert SILVERBERG
LORD VALENTINE'S CASTLE
(Valentine seeks to regain rulership over large, diverse planetwide society)

▷ Hal CLEMENT
MISSION OF GRAVITY
(a discus-shaped planet where gravity is up to 700 times Earth normal at the poles)

▷ J G BALLARD
HELLO AMERICA
(the desert wastelands of an America devastated by the energy crisis)

▷ Bruce STERLING
INVOLUTION OCEAN
(sailing the ocean of dust on the waterless world of Nullaqua)

Harsh Environments

▷ Ursula K LEGUIN
THE LEFT HAND OF DARKNESS
(life and society on the winter world Gethen, and the tribulations of an alien envoy)

▷ Philip K DICK
MARTIAN TIME-SLIP
(colonists struggle to survive in the neglected settlements of Mars)

Mack REYNOLDS
LOOKING BACKWARDS, FROM THE YEAR 2000
(set in a realistic socialist utopia)

▷ John BRUNNER
THE JAGGED ORBIT
(the Mafia and military-industrial complex, merged into one vast organisation)

L Neil SMITH
THE PROBABILITY BROACH
(an alternate world dominated by an anarchist form of capitalism – described in considerable detail)

▷ Frederik POHL and
▷ C M KORNBLUTH
GLADIATOR-AT-LAW
(boardroom battles in a socially divided capitalist near future where two ancient multibillionaires effectively control the economic system)

▷ Isaac ASIMOV
THE MARTIAN WAY
(short novel about Martian colonists struggling against economic sanctions applied by Earth, in parallel of revolutionary US – in the collection of the same name)

Damon KNIGHT
A FOR ANYTHING
(explores the economic effects of the invention of a matter duplicator)

Economics

supervised by the cynical Harshaw; it proceeds to the extent of Smith's founding a religion teaching the Martians' cultural values and lifestyle. Unsurprisingly, America is not yet ready for the heretical ethos of free love and self-administered justice that he preaches. Despite certain lapses of credibility and coherence, *Stranger* remains one of the most famous şf satires.

Heinlein's other books include The Door Into Summer *(a fast moving time travel story),* The Moon Is A Harsh Mistress *(a story of rebellion in an exploited lunar colony), the children's books* The Star Beast *and* Have Space-Suit, Will Travel, *and* The Puppet Masters *(a cheerfully paranoid novel about invasion by alien parasites). His later work is well represented by* Friday *and the lightly comic* Job.

READ·ON   ▶   John Boyd, *The Last Starship From Earth*
      ▷ Jerry Pournelle, *King David's Spaceship*
      ▷ Joe Haldeman, *Worlds*
      ▷ Gordon R Dickson, *The Outposter*
    ▶ To Heinlein's politics:
      ▷ Larry Niven, *Protector*
        Ayn Rand, *Atlas Shrugged*
    ▶ To his stories for adolescents:
      ▷ James Blish, *Mission To The Heart Stars*
        Alexei Panshin, *Rite Of Passage*
    ▶ To the short stories:
      ▷ John Brunner, *No Future In It*

HERBERT, Frank (1920–86)
US novelist and short story writer

Herbert approaches his overriding concerns, the logic of intelligence and its relation to our perceptions of reality, through the depiction of alien forms of humanity (as in *Hellstrom's Hive*, 1973, about a society of genetically altered humans who have patterned themselves on the insect hive, in the process losing much of their individuality) and of sentient non-humans (for example in *Whipping Star*, 1970, and its sequel *The Dosadi Experiment*, 1977, which deal with a 'Consentiency' of intelligent beings, from living stars to the utterly alien Gowachin whose judicial system puts everyone in the court on trial). Also characteristic of Herbert's writing is his distrust of machinery in favour of highly trained or specially adapted natural organisms (often possessing superhuman abilities). This is particularly apparent in *The Dosadi Experiment* (which explores the consequences of a hideous project in forced evolution) and in *The God Makers* (1972), which makes Herbert's underlying mysticism explicit in its story of a god made by human efforts.

DUNE (1965–85)

The Dune novels were intended as a survey of thousands of years of human history, mapping out the evolutionary changes in humanity as it moves towards an ideal state. Regrettably, Herbert died after only half the series was complete. Nevertheless the brilliant *Dune,* the first book, is fully readable on its own. It describes the arrival of Paul Atreides on the harsh desert world of Dune, and his assumption of the role of messiah to its warrior natives. The book's strength lies in its superbly detailed background: a feudal galactic empire dominated by many conflicting power groups, from the secret matriarchy of the Bene Gesserit to the barely human members of the Spacing Guild. All these forces vie for control of the spice melange, which brings long life and the power of prophecy – and of which Dune is the only source. The novel is also a searching examination of the roots of religion, full of insight and moral ambiguities. In the later Dune books (*Dune Messiah, Children Of Dune, God-Emperor Of Dune, Heretics Of Dune* and *Chapter House Dune*), despite a distinct falling off of inventiveness and a tendency towards opaque and difficult prose, Herbert expands on the themes of the first book, jumping thousands of years into the future.

Herbert's other books include The Green Brain *(about mutated insects which fight back against ecological disaster),* The Santaroga Barrier *(describing an isolated group of humans who have achieved a higher order of sentience),* The Dragon In The Sea *(a study of the psychological pressures on board a deep-diving submarine in a future war),* Destination: Void *(concerned with the nature of artificial intelligence),* The Eyes Of Heisenberg, The Heaven Makers, The Jesus Incident *(with Bill Ransom),* Soul Catcher *(non-sf, but related) and* Eye *(collection).*

READ·ON

▶ To *Dune*'s evolutionary concerns:
▷ Gordon Dickson, *The Final Encyclopedia*
▶ To his biological invention:
▷ Brian Stableford, *Wildeblood's Empire*
▷ Cordwainer Smith, *Norstrilia*
▷ Bruce Sterling, *Schismatrix*
   T J Bass, *Half Past Human*
   M A Foster, *The Gameplayers Of Zan*
▶ To his examinations of perception:
▷ Ian Watson, *The Embedding*
▷ Brian Aldiss, *Barefoot In The Head*

THE HERO AS VILLAIN
▷ Iain Banks, *The Wasp Factory*
▷ Alfred Bester, *Tiger! Tiger!*

▷ Stephen Donaldson, *The Chronicles Of Thomas Covenant*
▷ K W Jeter, *Dr Adder*
▷ Michael Moorcock, *Stormbringer*
▷ Norman Spinrad, *The Men In The Jungle*

HESSE, Hermann (1877–1962)
German/Swiss novelist

Hesse, recipient of the Nobel Prize for Literature, in his later work explores the nature of reality and the correct approach to life (balanced between our intellectual and sensual selves) through sf-related images and metaphors. *The Glass Bead Game* (1943; translated 1960), describes an academic community centred around the abstract game of the title. The protagonist, who as Master of the Game holds the most exalted position in the community, nevertheless discovers that a life of cerebral abstraction cannot offer ultimate fulfilment.

READ•ON
● *Steppenwolf* also uses fantastic imagery. *Narziss And Goldmund*
▶ To setting:
▷ Brian Aldiss, *The Malacia Tapestry*
▷ Mervyn Peake, *Titus Groan*
▶ To theme:
▷ Thomas Pynchon, *The Crying Of Lot 49*
▷ John Crowley, *Aegypt*

HOLDSTOCK, Robert (born 1948)
British novelist and short story writer

Holdstock's first novel, *Eye Among The Blind* (1976), was interesting hard sf, but with his second, *Earthwind* (1977), drawing on Irish culture and myth, he began to make a real impression. The latter prefigures the subtle, resonant *Mythago Wood* (1985), which describes a small, ancient forest, where 'myth imagos' from prehuman legends to modern folk-myths take on real form – and, inevitably, so do the myths. Jealousy over a beautiful girl from the wood, herself a mythago, leads the two main characters into the Heartwood, where the bloody resolution of the legend must be played out.

READ•ON
● *Lavondyss* (the sequel to *Mythago Wood*)
▶ ▷ Alan Garner, *Red Shift*
▷ Guy Gavriel Kay, *The Summer Tree*

HORROR AND GOTHIC
▷ Iain Banks, *The Wasp Factory*
▷ Clive Barker, *The Books Of Blood*
　Ramsey Campbell, *Dark Feasts*
　James Herbert, *The Rats*
　Shirley Jackson, *We Have Always Lived In The Castle*
▷ Stephen King, *The Shining*
▷ H P Lovecraft, *The Haunter Of The Dark*
▷ Edgar Allan Poe, *Tales Of Mystery And Imagination*
▷ Mary Shelley, *Frankenstein*
　Bram Stoker, *Dracula*

HOWARD, Robert E (1906–1936)
US novelist and short story writer

Credit for the invention of the sword and sorcery genre is usually given to Howard, on the basis of his creation of such characters as the archetypal tough barbarian Conan, who hacks his way across a prehistoric world full of evil wizards and persuasible princesses. Apart from such entirely Howard-written books as *Conan The Conqueror* (1950), the hero's popularity has ensured that most available collections (such as *Conan The Freebooter,* 1968) are partially or wholly pastiche, written by later imitators.

READ·ON
● *Almuric*
▶ ▷ de Camp and Nyberg, *Conan The Avenger,* one of the better pastiches
▶ ▷ Lin Carter, *The Warrior Of World's End*
　C L Moore, *Jirel Of Joiry* is similar, but has a female hero
◊ Sword and Sorcery

HOYLE, Fred (born 1915)
British novelist and short story writer

An astronomer by profession, Hoyle has written a considerable quantity of sf, both on his own and in collaboration with his son Geoffrey. In most of his work his fascination with science and the scientific method is clearly visible, the technical background details being given to the reader with a convincing and authoritative air. While enthusiasm for technical accuracy tends to overshadow his characters – generally unemotional but intelligent young scientists – he remains one of the better writers of 'hard' science fiction. Hoyle's best-known novel, *The Black Cloud* (1957), is a story of first contact with a totally alien intelligence, a sentient dustcloud which enters the Solar System and begins to approach Earth. The novel centres on a group of scientists who are trying both to communicate with the cloud and to quell the not inconsiderable public alarm as it envelops Earth, blocking out the sun. The difficulties faced by the scientists, their investigative methods and their eventual rewards are all described with the combination of meticulous detail and gusto which is typical of Hoyle.

READ•ON
- *October The First Is Too Late* (set on an Earth where many historical periods exist simultaneously)
  Fifth Planet (Soviets and Westerners mount missions to an alien planet); *Rockets In Ursa Major* (space opera with scientist as hero), both with Geoffrey Hoyle
- ▶ James P Hogan, *Inherit The Stars*
- ▶ Related stories of alien contact:
  - ▷ Arthur C Clarke, *Rendezvous With Rama*
  - ▷ Gregory Benford, *In The Ocean Of Night*

HUBBARD, L(afayette) Ron (1911–86)
US novelist and short story writer

Hubbard was a forceful proponent of 'real' sf – by which he meant the classic pulp action-adventure style. *Battlefield Earth* (1987) rivals ▷ E E Smith for characterisation, ▷ Norman for sensitivity, ▷ van Vogt for coherence, ▷ Howard for literary sensibility. It is set in Hubbard's vision of a world of the year 3000, populated by Scotsmen who always wear kilts and aliens evocatively known as Psychlos; a planet whose atmosphere explodes on contact with uranium; organisms whose nerves are big enough to attach tags to. Hubbard's imagination boils over on every page. A selection of forewords and prefaces, among them the translator's apology for his excessive use of Earth cliché, gets Hubbard's awesome, ten-volume *rara avis Mission Earth: The Biggest Science Fiction Dekalogy Ever Written* (1986–8) off to a flying start. No short description can really communicate the sheer scale of Hubbard's magnum opus, or the uncritical joy it takes from the classic pulp ethos – warts and all. *Mission Earth: The Biggest Science Fiction Dekalogy Ever Written* promises the reader thrills, spills, tension, satire and wacky parody; with its unparalleled levels of style, invention, and research, it must surely stand as one of the biggest dekalogies science fiction has ever produced, a truly gargantuan fictional erection.

READ•ON
- ▶ ▷ Robert A Heinlein, *Friday*
  Perry Rhodan 1, Enterprise Stardust

Edmond Hamilton, *Captain Future And The Space Emperor*

HUGO AWARD WINNERS

(The Science Fiction Achievement Awards, universally known as 'Hugos', are voted on by the members of the annual World Science Fiction Convention. Awards are made in a number of categories; we only list winners in the novel category.)

1953: ▷ Alfred Bester, *The Demolished Man*
1954: no award
1955: Mark Clifton and Frank Riley, *They'd Rather Be Right*
1956: ▷ Robert A Heinlein, *Double Star*
1957: no award
1958: ▷ Fritz Leiber, *The Big Time*
1959: ▷ James Blish, *A Case Of Conscience*
1960: ▷ Robert A Heinlein, *Starship Troopers*
1961: ▷ Walter M Miller, *A Canticle For Leibowitz*
1962: ▷ Robert A Heinlein, *Stranger In A Strange Land*
1963: ▷ Philip K Dick, *The Man In The High Castle*
1964: ▷ Clifford Simak, *Way Station*
1965: ▷ Fritz Leiber, *The Wanderer*
1966: ▷ Roger Zelazny . . . *And Call Me Conrad* and ▷ Frank Herbert, *Dune* (tie)
1967: ▷ Robert A Heinlein, *The Moon Is A Harsh Mistress*
1968: ▷ Roger Zelazny, *Lord Of Light*
1969: ▷ John Brunner, *Stand On Zanzibar*
1970: ▷ Ursula K LeGuin, *The Left Hand Of Darkness*
1971: ▷ Larry Niven, *Ringworld*
1972: ▷ Philip José Farmer, *To Your Scattered Bodies Go*
1973: ▷ Isaac Asimov, *The Gods Themselves*
1974: ▷ Arthur C Clarke, *Rendezvous With Rama*
1975: ▷ Ursula K LeGuin, *The Dispossessed*
1976: ▷ Joe Haldeman, *The Forever War*
1977: ▷ Kate Wilhelm, *Where Late The Sweet Birds Sang*
1978: ▷ Frederik Pohl, *Gateway*
1979: ▷ Vonda N McIntyre, *Dreamsnake*
1980: ▷ Arthur C Clarke, *The Fountains Of Paradise*
1981: Joan Vinge, *The Snow Queen*
1982: ▷ C J Cherryh, *Downbelow Station*
1983: ▷ Isaac Asimov, *Foundation's Edge*
1984: ▷ David Brin, *Startide Rising*
1985: ▷ William Gibson, *Neuromancer*
1986: ▷ Orson Scott Card, *Ender's Game*
1987: ▷ Orson Scott Card, *Speaker For The Dead*

1988: ▷ David Brin, *The Uplift War*

HUMOUR AND PARODY
▷ Douglas Adams, *The Hitch-Hiker's Guide To The Galaxy*
▷ Poul Anderson, *The Makeshift Rocket*
▷ Thomas M Disch, *The Businessman*
▷ Harry Harrison, *Bill, The Galactic Hero*
  Barry Hughart, *Bridge Of Birds*
  John Jakes, *Mention My Name In Atlantis*
  Keith Laumer, *Retief's Ransom*
▷ Stanislaw Lem, *The Cyberiad*
▷ Terry Pratchett, *The Colour Of Magic*
▷ John Sladek, *Tik-Tok*

HUXLEY, Aldous (1894–1963)
British novelist

Huxley was best known during his early career for mainstream writing; novels such as *Point Counter Point, Crome Yellow* and *Antic Hay* cynically derided between-wars preoccupations and weaknesses. *After Many A Summer* (1939) uses a longevity drug and its effects to make points about humans' essential bestiality, a theme also dealt with in *Ape And Essence* (1948), a grim dystopian treatment of social and moral reversion. *Brave New World* (1932), while set in an Earthly future, should not be read as straightforward prophecy. Huxley was fundamentally a moral writer, and in his masterpiece he fiercely attacks his contemporaries' obsession with the release of indulgence. In the World State, the breeding of low-intelligence clones (their brains soaked in alcohol during test-tube gestation) for the menial tasks of society means that the more fortunate are free to indulge their leisure appetites – with 'feelies' (pan-sensory movies), religious orgies at which Henry Ford is worshipped, and the ever-present 'soma', a euphoric drug. Huxley attacks the sterility and bestiality of this society through the character of the naïve Savage, brought up on an isolated Reservation; but it is defended by Mustafa Mond, the World Controller, who points out that everyone is perfectly happy and ideally suited (by infant conditioning) to their niche in life.

READ·ON
● *Island* (a contrasting utopia)
  The Doors Of Perception/Heaven And Hell (paired essays on hallucinogenic perception and on the afterlife)
▶ ▷ Robert A Heinlein, *Stranger In A Strange Land*
  B F Skinner, *Walden Two*
  ▷ Harry Harrison, *Homeworld*
◊ Future Societies

I

IMMORTALITY AND EXTENDED LIFE
▷ Orson Scott Card, *Capitol*
▷ Robert A Heinlein, *Methuselah's Children*
▷ Aldous Huxley, *After Many A Summer*
▷ Michael Moorcock, *The Dancers At The End Of Time*
▷ Kim Stanley Robinson, *Icehenge*
▷ Robert Silverberg, *The Book Of Skulls*
▷ Clifford Simak, *Way Station*
▷ Bruce Sterling, *Schismatrix*
▷ John Wyndham, *Trouble With Lichen*
▷ Roger Zelazny, *Lord Of Light*

INTELLIGENCE INCREASE
▷ Poul Anderson, *Brainwave*
▷ John Brunner, *The Stone That Never Came Down*
▷ Thomas M Disch, *Camp Concentration*
▷ Daniel Keyes, *Flowers For Algernon*
  Wilmar Shiras, *Children Of The Atom*
▷ Olaf Stapledon, *Sirius*

J

JETER, K W (born 1950)
US novelist

Jeter is an anti-intellectual intellectual, a thoughtful writer who despises the apparatus of academic criticism. His major sf work is a 'thematic trilogy' examining aspects of modern America by projecting them into the near future. It begins with *Dr Adder* (1987), an extremely powerful novel featuring aberrant sexuality, alien contact and the media, and is continued in *The Glass Hammer* (1985), a more considered work dealing with religion and ultimate reality, and *Death Arms* (1987).

READ·ON ● *Infernal Devices* (Victorian fantasy)
Seeklight (one of the horror novels Jeter regards as the other half of his work)

► ▷ William Burroughs, *The Naked Lunch*
  ▷ Harlan Ellison, *Deathbird Stories*
► To *The Glass Hammer*:
  ▷ Philip K Dick, *The Man In The High Castle*

JONES, Gwyneth (born 1952)
British novelist and short story writer

As Ann Halam, Jones has produced a number of excellent juvenile fantasies (such as *King Death's Garden,* 1986), while her adult fiction appears under her own name. *Divine Endurance* (1985) is a novel of political intrigue combining Buddhist philosophy with a feminist consciousness, set far in our future. *Escape Plans* (1986) is about all forms of escape: physical escape, freedom from one's own ingrained prejudices, Christian transcendence and evasion of the limitations of the physical universe, described against the background of an 'information society' reminiscent of ▷ Gibson.

READ·ON ► To *Divine Endurance*:
  Mark S Geston, *Lords Of The Starship*
► To *Escape Plans*:
  ▷ John Brunner, *The Shockwave Rider*

JUVENILES
  L Frank Baum, *The Wonderful Wizard Of Oz*
▷ John Christopher, *The White Mountains*
  Susan Cooper, *The Dark Is Rising*
  Michael de Larrabeiti, *The Borribles*
  Peter Dickinson, *The Weathermonger*
  Michael Ende, *The Neverending Story*
▷ Alan Garner, *Elidor*
▷ Robert A Heinlein, *Have Space Suit, Will Travel*
▷ C S Lewis, *The Magician's Nephew*
▷ Diana Wynne Jones, *Wilkins' Tooth*

K

KAFKA, Franz (1883–1924)
Czech novelist and short story writer

Kafka's dream-like fables are surrealist allegories examining authority, religion and the human response to our perception of the universe. To those with an appropriate sense of humour, they are also very funny. In *The Trial* (1925), for example, a vaguely defined protagonist (known only as K) wanders through a senseless and sinister bureaucracy attempting to discover what crime he has been accused of committing, and how to defend himself against charges which no one will define for him.

R E A D • O N
●   *The Castle*
▶ ▷ Stanislaw Lem, *Memoirs Found In A Bathtub*
▷ Iain Banks, *The Bridge*
▷ Philip K Dick, *Flow My Tears, The Policeman Said*

KAY, Guy Gavriel
US novelist

The Summer Tree, the first volume of the *Fionavar Tapestry* (1985–87), draws on a number of mythological sources – occasionally in a rather slap-dash manner – to endow its ▷ Tolkienesque adventure story with resonant, emotive imagery. The characters' sufferings are vividly described, the effect only slightly marred by Kay's rather wooden style, and the protagonists are sufficiently well-drawn to make the reader really feel for them in the ordeals they must go through in their quest to save Fionavar from its ultimate enemy. *The Wandering Fire* and *The Darkest Road* complete the trilogy.

R E A D • O N
▶ Megan Lindholm, *Wizard Of The Pigeons*
▷ Michael Moorcock, *Stormbringer*

KEYES, Daniel
US novelist and short story writer

Flowers For Algernon (1966) is the story of Charlie Gordon, whose low IQ and willingness to learn make him an ideal subject for the surgical increase of his mental powers; the medical staff, however, see him only as an object of scientific curiosity. Algernon, the mouse on whom the technique was 'perfected', loses his intelligence and dies, and Charlie, realising that he, too, will inevitably regress, can only attempt to finish his own research on the process before he loses his faculties. His diary entries as he feels his intelligence draining away are deeply moving, carrying a devastating emotional charge.

R E A D • O N
●   *The Fifth Sally*
▶ ▷ Robert Silverberg, *Dying Inside*
◊   Intelligence Increase

KING, Stephen (born 1946)
US novelist

King is famous for such bestselling horror novels as *The Shining* and *Salem's Lot*, many of which have been filmed. *Firestarter* (1980), *The Dead Zone* (1979) and *Carrie* (1974) all deal with the standard sf theme of paranormal mental powers. Each tells the story of a person (child, adult and adolescent respectively) gifted with such a power, and their treatment by the rest of society. All King's books are exciting and readable, and in these three the tense plot is combined with a real feeling for the way the characters are tormented and endangered through being different. More recently, *The Eyes of the Dragon* (1986) has a classic fairy story plot and *The Tommyknockers* (1988) concerns UFOs.

READ · ON
- ● *Different Seasons* (collection)
  The Running Man
- ▶ Stories of freaks rejected by society:
  - ▷ Robert Silverberg, *Dying Inside*
  - ▷ John Wyndham, *The Chrysalids*
  - ▷ Theodore Sturgeon, *More Than Human*

KORNBLUTH, C(yril) M (1923–58)
US novelist and short story writer

Although best known for his collaboration with ▷ Frederik Pohl on *The Space Merchants,* Kornbluth produced equally cynical and satiric work on his own, as in *The Syndic* (1953), describing a utopian form of gangster rule. However, his most memorable works are his short stories. Whether compassionately observing the underdogs of society ('The Little Black Bag', 'The Altar At Midnight') or passing sardonic comment on humanity ('The Silly Season', 'The Marching Morons'), his status as one of America's finest and most acerbic short story writers in the genre is beyond dispute.

READ · ON
- ● *The Best Of Cyril Kornbluth* includes all the above stories
- ▶ ▷ Karel Čapek, *War With The Newts*
  - ▷ John Sladek, *Tik-Tok*

KURTZ, Katherine (born 1944)
US trilogist

Most of Kurtz's work deals with Gwynedd, a fictional analogue of medieval Wales distinguished by slight variations in hierarchy, geography (as manifest on the books' various maps), and racial distinctions. Besides short stories set there, she has written three trilogies and plans to write at least three more. The books show extensive knowledge of medieval history; the psychic Deryni supply an element of fantasy. The trilogies *The Chronicles Of The Deryni* (1970–3) and *The Histories Of King Kelson* (1984–6) are set when ordinary humanity is beginning to end its long persecution of the Deryni, while *The Legends Of Camber Of Culdi* (1976–81) describes the origin of the conflict. *Camber The Heretic* is the last book in the Camber trilogy. After the Restoration of the fully human line of Haldane kings with Cinhil, resentment appears against the Deryni who had ruled for so long, and a backlash occurs as Deryni-haters achieve power in court and church. When, after Cinhil's death, the Deryni Camber is elected Archbishop in preference to the Council's candidate, he is forced to flee and the Deryni religious orders are destroyed. This leads to the revocation of Camber's sainthood, the prohibition of Deryni priests, and a wave of popular hatred against the Deryni.

READ·ON ▶ ▷ Stephen Donaldson, *Mordant's Need*
　　　　　　　 ▷ Anne McCaffrey, *Dragonflight*
　　　　　　　　 Geraldine Harris, *Prince Of The Godborn*

KUTTNER, Henry (1915–58)
US novelist and short story writer

Frequently working in collaboration with his wife, C L Moore, and often using the pseudonym Lewis Padgett, Kuttner was one of the most inventive authors of his time. The unique blend of humour and rigorous logic that marks his short stories is at its most noticeable in his work about Galloway Gallegher, a drunken amnesiac inventor (collected in *Robots Have No Tails*, 1952), while his attitude towards robots makes an interesting contrast to ▷ Asimov's. His most memorable story, dealing with psi powers and hallucination, is 'The Fairy Chessmen' (in *The Chessboard Planet*, 1951).

READ·ON ● 　*Fury* (one man's struggle to drive humanity to conquer the surface of Venus)
　　　　　　　 ▶ ▷ Robert Sheckley, *Options*
　　　　　　　　 ▷ Avram Davidson, *Or All The Seas With Oysters*

L

LAFFERTY, R(aphael) A(loysius) (born 1914)
US novelist and short story writer

Lafferty's flamboyant style and fractured narratives place him among the most distinctive of the New Wave authors. His rich parables and tales jumble together gods, demons and ordinary mortals; *Nine Hundred Grandmothers* (1970) contains many of the best of his shorter pieces. Although his eccentric storytelling methods work less well in his novels, *Past Master* (Thomas More resurrected to save a utopia, 1968) and *Space Chantey* (Homer's Odyssey as space opera, 1968) are nevertheless remarkable.

R E A D • O N

- ● *Aurelia*
  Arrive At Easterwine
- ▶ ▷ Kurt Vonnegut, *The Sirens Of Titan*
- ▷ Avram Davidson, *The Enquiries Of Doctor Esterhazy*

THE LANDSCAPE AS HERO
- ▷ J G Ballard, *The Crystal World*
- ▷ M John Harrison, *Viriconium Nights*
  Jaime and Gilbert Hernandez, *The Return Of Mr X* (graphic novel)
- ▷ Michael Moorcock, *A Cure For Cancer*
- ▷ Mervyn Peake, *Gormenghast*

LEADERS
- John Calvin Batchelor, *The Birth Of The People's Republic Of Antarctica*
- ▷ James Branch Cabell, *Figures Of Earth*
- ▷ Philip K Dick, *The World Jones Made*
- ▷ Gordon R Dickson, *Dorsai!*
- ▷ Stephen Donaldson, *The Illearth War*
- ▷ Frank Herbert, *Dune Messiah*
- ▷ Tanith Lee, *The Storm Lord*
  Philip Mann, *Master Of Paxwax*

LEE, Tanith (born 1947)
British novelist and short story writer

Lee's novels show an understanding of both people and magic which is rare is genre fantasy. Her gift for creating psychologically acute and emotionally disturbing magical images is amply demonstrated in such stories as *Volkhavaar* (1977), an adult treatment of sorcery and true love, or 'Red As Blood', in which Snow White is a vampire and the 'wicked queen' a devout Christian (in the collection of inverted fairy-tales *Red As Blood*, 1983). *The Birthgrave* (1975) bases its 'magic' on psionics in its story of an amnesiac sorceress' quest for identity and freedom. *Cyrion* (1982), contrastingly, is an amusing novel about a hero who overcomes his adversaries by outwitting them rather than by brute force. *Death's Master* is one of a group of books set in a time when the Earth was flat, whose background (based on Arabic legends) is vividly evoked. The novel is full of powerful inventions, from the queen cursed to have children by no living man who therefore mates with a reanimated corpse, to the magical assassin which can be escaped only by destroying it every night, each time in a different way. It is alternately amusing, erotic and horrifying. Other Flat Earth books include *Night's Master* (1977) and *Night's Sorceries* (collection, 1987).

READ·ON
- ● *The Electric Forest* (sf)
  The Storm Lord
  Dreams Of Dark And Light (collection)
- ▶ Seamus Cullen, *A Noose Of Light*
  Jane Gaskell, *The Serpent*
- ▷ Michael Moorcock, *Stormbringer*
- ▶ To Lee's sf:
  Lisa Tuttle, *A Spaceship Built Of Stone*

LEGUIN, Ursula K(roeber) (born 1929)
US novelist and short story writer

LeGuin's early work, such as *Rocannon's World* (1966), is strongly romantic in tone, employing the rhythmically poetic prose which became her trademark, while later novels like *The Word For World Is Forest* (1972), a powerful Vietnam allegory set on an alien world, deal with deeper sociological themes. Most of LeGuin's sf is set in a common far future, in which all human worlds are allied to a Galaxy-wide Ekumen, a benevolent organisation which co-ordinates and assists in the flow of knowledge, rather than ruling. Each novel in the framework is set on a different planet: feudal in *Rocannon's World,* anarcho-communist in *The Dispossessed* (1974: a powerful study of a society which some readers regard as utopian, others as dystopian, set against an opposing description of a world dominated by capitalism). Her most important fantasy work, the 'juvenile' Earthsea trilogy (*A Wizard Of Earthsea*, *The Tombs Of Atuan* and *The Farthest Shore*, 1968–73), is richer in theme and character than most adult fantasy. It relates the theory and practice of magic in the world of Earthsea to Taoist notions of symmetry and naming, a concern echoed in the yin/yang structure of *The Dispossessed* and in *The Lathe Of Heaven* (1971), which describes attempts to manipulate a man whose dreams can alter reality.

THE LEFT HAND OF DARKNESS (1969)

Gethen, an ice-age planet, has a pre-industrial civilisation of bisexual human-oids. A young man called Genly Ai visits the planet as an ambassador of the Ekumen, trying to persuade the Gethenians to join the League of Known Worlds, but he and his mission become caught up in political and diplomatic intrigues between two opposed regimes. Eventually Genly is forced to flee for his life with Lord Estraven, an enigmatic politician in whose veiled character the Earthman seeks for the key to the Gethenian soul. The novel is written as Genly's report, interspersed with folktales, factual essays and Estraven's diary; this technique never interrupts the flow of the story, which is told in LeGuin's usual fluent and graceful style. Together the various elements present a full picture of an alien society unaffected by the gender differences which shape human lives.

LeGuin's other works include City Of Illusions, Planet Of Exile, Malafrena *(a realistic novel set in an alternate version of nineteenth century Europe),* Always Coming Home, *a vast pseudo-factual study of a utopian tribe living in a pastoral future California, and* Threshold, *a fantasy for adolescents about adolescence.*

READ·ON

● *The Wind's Twelve Quarters* (a collection including such excellent stories as 'The Ones Who Walk Away From Omelas', a fantasy parable which explores the morality of making a small minority suffer for the good of the majority)

▶ ▷ Michael Bishop, *A Funeral For The Eyes Of Fire*

▷ Mary Gentle, *Golden Witchbreed*

▷ Bob Shaw, *The Ragged Astronauts*

▷ Robert Silverberg, *A Time Of Changes*

▶ To the Taoism:

▷ Gregory Benford, *The Stars In Shroud*

▷ Norman Spinrad, *Songs From The Stars*

◊ Aliens and Alien Societies

◊ Future Societies

Ursula K LEGUIN ● *The Left Hand Of Darkness*

Charlotte Perkins GILMAN
HERLAND
*(classic in which male explorers find
utopian all-female society in mountains)*

▷ Theodore STURGEON
VENUS PLUS X
*(how an ordinary man reacts to a utopia of
hermaphrodites)*

▷ Joanna RUSS
THE FEMALE MAN
*(two different all-female societies: one
near-utopia, one locked in a savage war
with the male half of the human race)*

Single-Sex Societies

Philip WYLIE
THE DISAPPEARANCE
*(women and men segregated into two
completely separate worlds)*

Suzy McKee CHARNAS
MOTHERLINES
*(unsentimental account of societies of
free women in a world where all men are
irredeemably evil)*

▷ Robert SILVERBERG
LORD VALENTINE'S CASTLE
*(Valentine travels across vast planet to
discover himself and regain his kingdom)*

Treks

▷ Gene WOLFE
THE BOOK OF THE NEW SUN
*(Severian's odyssey across a dying Earth
takes him from boyhood to maturity)*

▷ Mervyn PEAKE
TITUS ALONE
*(the third Titus book, in which he leaves
Gormenghast – and childhood – behind)*

▷ Philip José FARMER
THE LOVERS
*(true love between a man and an –
apparently – humanoid woman)*

▷ James TIPTREE Jr
UP THE WALLS OF THE WORLD
*(ESP researchers contact aliens trying
to escape the impending destruction of
their world)*

Human/Alien Relationships

▷ Thomas M DISCH
MANKIND UNDER THE LEASH
*(aliens feed and care for humans like pets
– and abandon them in the same way)*

▷ Frank HERBERT
WHIPPING STAR
*(sentient star falls in love with the human
assigned to guard it)*

▷ Naomi MITCHISON
MEMOIRS OF A SPACEWOMAN
*('contact' specialist becomes empathically
close to various aliens)*

LEIBER, Fritz (born 1910)
US novelist and short story writer

Although Leiber demonstrates a greater affection for fantasy, he has written several excellent sf novels, including *Gather, Darkness!* (an amusing and ingenious story of superscience disguised as religion and witchcraft, 1950) and *The Wanderer* (a tale of global disaster also concerned with humanity's cosmic insignificance, 1964). His most famous sf work, however, is *The Big Time* (1961), part of a series about a 'Change War' fought for unknown masters by resurrected intermediaries, with the aim of changing the past to eliminate the enemy. The novel is notable for its depictions of human soldiers from the war, who move from poses of rebellion and independence to a gung-ho hollowness. Leiber's fantasy 'Swords' series recounts the adventures of the cheerful rogues Fafhrd and the Grey Mouser in the bizarre and unpredictable world of Nehwon. In *The Swords Of Lankhmar* we meet, among many other things, the hideous and crotchety Gods of Lankhmar, the sexual peculiarities of its Overlord Glipkerio, and a subterranean civilisation of intelligent rats. As always in the series, the story is told in a baroque and idiosyncratic manner, with a heavy dose of irony.

READ·ON

●   *A Pail Of Air* (collection)
    Conjure Wife (about a suburban witch)
    The Silver Eggheads (satire on the publishing industry)
    Swords Against Wizardry
▶   To the fantasy:
    ▷ L Sprague de Camp and Fletcher Pratt, *The Incomplete Enchanter*
    ▷ James Branch Cabell, *The Silver Stallion*
▶   To *The Wanderer*:
    ▷ John Brunner, *The Sheep Look Up*
▶   To *Gather, Darkness!*:
    ▷ Robert A Heinlein, *Sixth Column*

LEM, Stanislaw (born 1921)
Polish novelist, short story writer and essayist

Our inability to find sure solutions or clear understanding in a universe which is ultimately unknowable has been Lem's constant theme, from the metaphysical detective story *The Investigation* (1959) to the scientific problems of *The Invincible* (1964). Combined with this is Lem's tentative faith in humanity as opposed to technological or ideological solutions to human misery (especially visible in the amusing 'cybernetic fairy tales' of *The Cyberiad*, 1965). Lem's scientific background is reflected in the tricks he plays with cosmology and cybernetics in *The Cyberiad* and *A Perfect Vacuum* (1979), a fascinating collection of intellectual games in the form of reviews of non-existent books. *Solaris* (1961) is Lem's most famous work, his strongest expression of the alien nature of the universe. A group of scientists occupies a space station in orbit around a planet covered by a strange sea, which they suspect to be sentient, though they cannot be sure. As they prod the sea with landing probes and radio waves, it dredges dead and imaginary people from their subconscious minds and places them aboard the station in apparently human form, tormenting and maddening the investigators for reasons at which they can only guess.

READ•ON
- ● *The Futurological Congress* (social satire)
- ▶ To the theme of the alien universe:
  - ▷ Gregory Benford, *Against Infinity*
  - ▷ Barry Malzberg, *Beyond Apollo*
- ▶ To Lem's humour:
  - ▷ Karel Čapek, *The Absolute At Large*
  - ▷ Frederik Pohl, *The Space Merchants*

LESSING, Doris (born 1919)
British/Rhodesian novelist

Lessing initially approached sf with *Memoirs Of A Survivor* (a gentle post-holocaust story, 1971) and *Briefing For A Descent Into Hell* (1975), about mental illness. *Shikasta* (1979), her first genre novel, begins the epic Canopus In Argos: Archives series. Shikasta is the sick planet Earth, overseen throughout its history by the spiritual Canopean and physical Sirian Empires, as they struggle against the unhealthy influence of the criminal planet Shammat. The grandeur of Lessing's metaphor is rendered on a more human scale in such sequels as *The Marriages Between Zones Three, Four And Five* (1980) and the viciously satirical *The Sentimental Agents In The Volyen Empire* (1983).

READ•ON
- ▶ ▷ Olaf Stapledon, *Last And First Men*
- ▶ Aliens also struggle for humanity's soul in
  - ▷ William Burroughs, *Nova Express*
  - ▷ Philip K Dick, *Radio Free Albemuth*

LEWIS, C(live) S(taples) (1898–1963)
British novelist

Lewis is best known, and best loved, for his children's books set in the magical world of Narnia. The first, *The Lion, The Witch And The Wardrobe* (1950), is characteristic of the series and its appealing imagery. The subsequent books are stronger, culminating in the atmospheric *The Magician's Nephew* (1955) and the disturbing *The Last Battle* (1956). The Christian allegory in Narnia is unobtrusive, as is the moral behind Lewis' unacknowledged masterpiece *Till We Have Faces, A Myth Retold* (1956): 'dark idolatry and pale enlightenment at war with each other and with vision', in his own words. The myth is that of Cupid and Psyche, the prose vivid and the novel compelling. Christianity is central to Lewis' science fiction trilogy *Out Of The Silent Planet, Voyage To Venus/Perelandra* and *That Hideous Strength* (1938–45), although this is no barrier to enjoyment by non-Christians. The opening book, in which Dr Ransom, a philologist, inadvertently travels to Mars, is the most accessible, resembling ▷ H G Wells' sf with added mysticism. In the slower and more graceful sequel, Ransom attempts to prevent the Fall recurring on Venus, the book's tension coming from Ransom's direct, face-to-face conflict with the Adversary. The last novel is the strongest: an earthy, almost Gothic story with Ransom at his most charismatic. Sympathetic protagonists, convincingly everyday evil (as in *The Last Battle*) and darkly evocative writing complement a plot which involves the exhumation of Merlin.

R E A D · O N   ▶ ▷ J R R Tolkien, *The Lord Of The Rings*
                      Charles Williams, *War In Heaven*
                ▷ James Blish, *A Case Of Conscience*
                      Salman Rushdie, *The Satanic Verses*

LINGUISTICS AND LANGUAGES
▷ Anthony Burgess, *A Clockwork Orange*
▷ Samuel R Delany, *Babel-17*
   Suzette Haden Elgin, *Native Tongue*
▷ George Orwell, *1984*
▷ Norman Spinrad, *The Void Captain's Tale*
▷ Jack Vance, *The Languages Of Pao*
▷ Ian Watson, *The Embedding*

LOVECRAFT, H(oward) P(hilips) (1890–1937)
US short story writer and novelist

Lovecraft's work is strongly reminiscent of ▷ Poe, particularly in its baroque atmosphere and sense of numbing inevitability and despair, portraying humans' destinies as completely beyond their control. His Cthulhu Mythos works are a series of linked stories and novels in which blasphemous monstrosities from beyond time and space, the Great Old Ones, seek to gain control of our world via the inspiration of crazed worshippers and the activities of powerful servitor creatures. Among the most striking are 'The Shadow Over Innsmouth', 'The Dunwich Horror', 'The Call Of Cthulhu' and *At The Mountains Of Madness* (1936); a good collection is *The Haunter Of*

The Dark (1963). Lovecraft's monstrously adjectival style has spawned a host of imitators, including Brian Lumley and August Derleth.

READ·ON ▶ Ramsey Campbell, *Cold Print*
Clark Ashton Smith, *Out Of Space And Time*
Robert Shea and ▷ Robert Anton Wilson, *Illuminatus!* (a rather different use of the Mythos background)

LYNN, Elizabeth A (born 1946)
US novelist and short story writer

Lynn's fantasy trilogy Chronicles of Tornor explores culture and tradition in a changing world. The first book, *Watchtower* (1979), traces the fortunes of the soldier Ryke after the fall of Tornor Keep. The story focuses on the dichotomy between the rigid northern society and the relatively egalitarian southern culture. These societies are treated in more detail in *The Dancers Of Arun* (1979, about a disabled youth who becomes a sorceror) and *The Northern Girl* (1980). Lynn's science fiction includes *The Sardonyx Net* (1981), a political novel set in a somewhat dystopian future society.

READ·ON ● *The Man Who Loved The Moon* (collection)
▶ ▷ C J Cherryh, *Downbelow Station*
▷ Mary Gentle, *Golden Witchbreed*

M

MACAVOY, R(oberta) A
Irish novelist

MacAvoy's writing escapes the confines of genre fantasy by using an explicitly Earthly setting, glorying in a powerful sense of atmosphere and enchantment. The trilogy *Damiano, Damiano's Lute* and *Raphael* (1983–4) describes the friendship of the archangel Raphael and the medieval Italian magician Damiano Delstrego. *Tea With The Black Dragon* (1983) draws parallels between computer wizardry and equally mystical magical disciplines; a Chinese dragon in human form helps a Zen Buddhist folk violinist find her daughter, a systems analyst mixed up in computer fraud.

READ·ON ● *Twisting The Rope* (the sequel to *Black Dragon*)

> *Grey Horse* (set in historical Ireland)
> ► To *Damiano*:
> ▷ Diana Wynne Jones, *The Magicians of Caprona*
> ► To *Black Dragon*:
> Barry Hughart, *Bridge of Birds*
> H R F Keating, *Zen There Was Murder*

MAGIC
▷ Robert Asprin, *Another Fine Myth*
Brian Bates, *The Way Of Wyrd*
▷ John Crowley, *Aegypt*
▷ L Sprague de Camp, *The Incomplete Enchanter*
Randall Garrett, *Too Many Magicians*
▷ Tanith Lee, *Death's Master*
▷ Ursula K LeGuin, *A Wizard Of Earthsea*
▷ Larry Niven, *The Magic Goes Away*
▷ Terry Pratchett, *The Colour Of Magic*
Fletcher Pratt, *The Well Of The Unicorn*

MALZBERG, Barry (born 1939)
US novelist and short story writer

Central to Malzberg's work is the use of sf images to convey messages of uncertainty and apocalypse, strongly tinged with satire. Many of his novels invert sf's traditionally optimistic view of certain themes. *The Falling Astronauts* (1971), for example, presents a version, exaggerated for the purposes of metaphor, of the Apollo programme in which the astronauts struggle against nameless existential terrors. Other books, such as *Overlay* (1972), explore the despair and alienation of ordinary people, here race track punters betrayed by an alien tipster.

READ·ON
● *Screen* (uses pornographic imagery to convey existential problems)
The Cross Of Fire
Herovit's World
Galaxies
► ▷ J G Ballard, *Crash*
▷ William Burroughs, *Nova Express*
► The novels of ▷ Philip K Dick, such as *The Simulacra,* use similar approaches to different themes

MAN/MACHINE INTEGRATION
▷ Algis Budrys, *Who?*
  Martin Caidin, *Cyborg/The Six Million Dollar Man*
  Keith Laumer, *A Plague Of Demons*
▷ Anne McCaffrey, *The Ship Who Sang*
▷ Vonda N McIntyre, *Superluminal*
▷ Frederik Pohl, *Man Plus*
▷ Rudy Rucker, *Software*
▷ John Sladek, *The Muller-Fokker Effect*

MARTIN, George R(aymond) R(ichard) (born 1948)
US novelist and short story writer

Martin's reputation rests mainly on his early short stories, which explore such traditional sf themes as telepathy and faster-than-light travel with exceptional intelligence and humanity. Many of these pieces deal with the confrontation between harsh reality and a beautiful illusion – 'The Way Of Cross And Dragon' (in *Sandkings*, 1981), for example, describes the inner conflicts of a roving inquisitor for a future Catholic Church who must deal with a heresy that brings its followers peace and happiness, while glorifying Judas Iscariot.

READ·ON   ● *A Song For Lya* (collection)
      Dying Of The Light
      Windhaven (with Lisa Tuttle)
  ▶ ▷ Poul Anderson, *The Queen Of Air And Dark-ness*
    ▷ James Tiptree Jr, *Brightness Falls From The Air*

MAY, Julian (born 1931)
US novelist

After publishing one novelette, the widely anthologised 'Dune Roller', in 1951, May published little further fiction until *The Many-Coloured Land* in 1982. She spent the intervening thirty years writing scientific articles on a range of subjects, and the scope of her interests is evident in the detailed settings and the specialised talents of the characters in her books. The psychic powers possessed by many of her characters are also convincingly portrayed, using vivid imagery to achieve emotional impact. *The Many-Coloured Land* is the first of four books constituting the Saga Of The Exiles. Misfits from the Galactic Milieu, a civilisation of intelligent alien races into which humanity has been inducted in our near future, pass through a one-way time gate into the Pliocene, six million years in the past, to find not the prehistoric paradise they had imagined but warring alien races who use the stranded humans to further their own ends. The personal oddities of the misfits add amusement and interest to the underlying power of the mythic archetypes on which many of the characters are based.

READ•ON ● *The Golden Torc, The Nonborn King* and *The Adversary* are the other three books. *A Pliocene Companion* provides such items as a character list and glossary. May's next work is to be a trilogy set in the Galactic Milieu itself, to which *Intervention* forms a link.

▶ ▷ Stephen Donaldson, *The Chronicles Of Thomas Covenant*

▷ Marion Zimmer Bradley, *The Heritage Of Hastur*

▷ Anne McCaffrey, *To Ride Pegasus*

MCCAFFREY, Anne (born 1926)
US novelist and short story writer

McCaffrey's fantasy novels combine adventure with romance, generally involving women in a more prominent role than is usual in such work. She is best known for collections of linked books and stories; these include the two Crystal Singer books and the collection *The Ship Who Sang* (1969). Among her other works are *Restoree* (1967), about a girl who finds herself in an unknown body on a different world, *Decision At Doona* (1969), a two-sided first contact novel, and *Get Off The Unicorn* (1977), a collection of stories set in several different worlds of McCaffrey's creation. Although her settings are boldly drawn, her characters, with their recognisable traits and emotions, dominate the books. McCaffrey's major work is a group of books set on Pern, a former colony world which lost contact with Earth several centuries before the opening of the series. *Dragonflight* (1968) introduces the reader to the Dragonriders, men and women who are telepathically linked with dragons and defend Pern from enemies both human and natural. ('Thread', deadly to all organic life, falls periodically from another planet.) Other books set on Pern are *Dragonquest* (1971), *The White Dragon* (1978) and *Moreta, Dragonlady Of Pern* (1983), set 400 years before *Dragonflight*.

READ•ON ● *Dragonsong* and its sequels (children's books set on Pern)
To Ride Pegasus (about near future psionic 'Talents')

> The Crystal Singer
> ► Doris Piserchia, *Star Rider*
> ▷ Andre Norton, *Witch World*
> ▷ Barbara Hambly, *The Time Of The Dark*

MCINTYRE, Vonda N(eel) (born 1948)
US novelist and short story writer

McIntyre's first story, the novelette 'Of Mist, And Grass, And Sand', was later expanded into the novel *Dreamsnake* (1978), whose protagonist is a healer and geneticist in a post-holocaust world more believable than most. *Superluminal* (1984) is the moving tale of a woman, made into a cyborg in order to pilot a spacecraft, who finds that she has lost the ability to take part in human relationships. McIntyre's short stories, gathered in *Fireflood* (1979), handle similar themes; her protagonists are usually distanced from society, often by physical disfigurement, and she invests them with a singular life and humanity.

READ•ON   ● *The Exile Waiting*
► ▷ Kate Wilhelm, *The Clewiston Test*
▷ Joanna Russ, *(Extra)Ordinary People*

MCKILLIP, Patricia A
US novelist

McKillip is best known for her imaginative fantasy stories, which skilfully blend magical powers with human elements. Her best work, *The Riddle-Master Of Hed* (1976), introduces the quest of Morgon, Prince of Hed, to unravel the mysteries of his own identity and destiny. Rather than being thoughtlessly grafted onto a feudal setting, the magic in Morgon's world is deeply connected with the nature of reality and forms the basis of a true 'divine right' of kings. The story continues in *Heir Of Sea And Fire* (1977) and *Harpist In The Wind* (1979). McKillip's best non-fantasy work is *Fool's Run* (1987), an sf novel stylistically similar to the books of ▷ C J Cherryh.

READ•ON   ● *The Forgotten Beasts Of Eld*
► Jo Clayton, *Moongather*
▷ Jack Vance, *Lyonesse*

MEDIA
▷ Algis Budrys, *Michaelmas*

▷ D G Compton, *The Continuous Katherine Mortenhoe*
▷ Philip K Dick, *Dr Bloodmoney*
   James Morrow, *The Continent Of Lies*
▷ Frederik Pohl and
▷ C M Kornbluth, *The Space Merchants*
▷ Keith Roberts, *Gráinne*
   Ali Sloss, *Rainbow's End*
▷ Norman Spinrad, *Bug Jack Barron*
▷ Bruce Sterling, *The Artificial Kid*

MENTAL DISORDER
▷ J G Ballard, *Crash*
▷ Iain Banks, *The Wasp Factory*
   Ramsey Campbell, *Incarnate*
▷ Philip K Dick, *Martian Time-Slip*
▷ Robert Sheckley, *The Alchemical Marriage Of Alistair Crompton*
▷ Gene Wolfe, *Soldier Of The Mist*

MESSIAHS
▷ Brian Aldiss, *Barefoot In The Head*
▷ John Barth, *Giles Goat-Boy*
▷ Philip K Dick, *The Three Stigmata Of Palmer Eldritch*
▷ Stephen Donaldson, *The Second Chronicles Of Thomas Covenant*
▷ Frank Herbert, *Dune Messiah*
   Langdon Jones and
▷ Michael Moorcock ed, *The Nature Of The Catastrophe*
▷ Michael Moorcock, *Behold The Man*
   Gore Vidal, *Messiah*
▷ Gene Wolfe, *The Book Of The New Sun*

MILLER, Walter M(ichael) born (1922)
US novelist and short story writer

Miller produced most of his work in the form of short stories such as 'The Darfsteller', a study of an unemployed actor who takes the place of one of his android successors for one last performance (in *The Darfsteller*, 1982). These pieces were largely overshadowed in the 1960s by the success of his novel *A Canticle For Leibowitz* (1960), (see below), the strongest expression of Miller's concern with the struggles of small groups of individuals to overcome the adverse effects of technology. His work is straightforward and direct, lacking in literary devices and flowery prose, but well-written and with a depth of characterisation that makes it stand out from the majority of the sf of its time. *A Canticle For Leibowitz* was one of the first books in sf to take religious belief as its subject. Set in southwest America after a nuclear holocaust, this thought-provoking novel details the growth of a new religious order around the few surviving personal effects of one Isaac Leibowitz, electrical engineer. Miller uses this scenario to examine the changing characters and motivations of the monks of the order of Leibowitz, as the hostile world around them develops and moves towards a new Renaissance, echoing the pattern of human history from the Dark Ages to modern times.

READ·ON ▶ To the themes of religion:
▷ Frank Herbert, *Dune*
▷ Philip K Dick, *A Maze Of Death*
▷ James Blish, *Black Easter*

MITCHISON, Naomi (born 1897)
British novelist and short story writer

Mitchison is chiefly a writer of historical fiction (often with fantasy elements), but has written several sf short stories and the novels *Memoirs Of A Spacewoman* (1962) and *Solution Three* (1975). *Memoirs,* a major work, is an ingenious novel of first contact told by a professional 'communicator' (one of the first examples of a strong female character in genre sf), presenting interesting and unusual perspectives on sex and biology. *Solution Three* depicts a future world where homosexuality has been adopted as the solution to problems of overpopulation.

READ·ON ▶ ▷ Orson Scott Card, *Speaker For The Dead*
▷ James Tiptree Jr, *The Starry Rift*
H Beam Piper, *Little Fuzzy*.

MOORCOCK, Michael (born 1939)
British editor, novelist and short story writer

Moorcock's first major contribution to speculative fiction was the early Elric stories (collected in *The Stealer Of Souls,* 1967 and the novel *Stormbringer,* 1965), sword and sorcery with a hero very different from the usual run: a Byronic hero-villain who fits the stories' dark, romantic mood. Though they were written primarily to entertain, there are deeper, more powerful, levels of meaning and symbolism, embedded in such inventions as Elric's sword, Stormbringer, which sucks souls from its victims. As in much of Moorcock's work, the landscapes are not physical but metaphysical, reflecting the unconscious feelings and desires of the protagonists. The Elric stories, like virtually all the rest of Moorcock's work, are set in the 'Multiverse', an assembly of many parallel universes, allowing interesting interconnections between otherwise entirely separate books. Many novels involve incarnations of the same hero (as in *The Eternal Champion,* 1970, *The Jewel In The Skull,* 1967, and *The Knight Of The Swords,* 1971, each of which begins a series). From 1964 to 1971 Moorcock edited the British sf magazine *New Worlds,* which sought to broaden the possibilities of the idiom and was a seminal influence in the British New Wave, encouraging new writers and experimental forms of writing. Recently Moorcock has moved into more conventional forms of fiction; *Byzantium Endures* (1981) and *The Laughter Of Carthage* (1984) echo the concerns of the Jerry Cornelius stories (see below) in their presentation of the prejudiced, arrogant and hypocritical Colonel Pyat, who has lived through many of the central events of the twentieth century.

THE CORNELIUS CHRONICLES (1965–77)

These novels and short stories, set in landscapes almost continually in the throes of entropic decay, are an attempt to express the essential concerns of their time, epitomising the 1960s (and, later, the whole of the twentieth century) in stories whose interpretation is as much the readers' affair as the author's. The Final Programme re-expresses the concerns of the early Elric tales in modern terms, while with *A Cure For Cancer* the narrative becomes more complex and in *The English Assassin* and *The Condition Of Muzak* it is strongly nonlinear. Deliberate whimsicalities are frequent, providing the books with an exceptionally rich texture in which no reader is expected to, nor needs to, grasp every detail. The four novels are now published in two omnibus volumes as *The Cornelius Chronicles.* Other authors became strongly involved with Jerry Cornelius, using Moorcock's characters in their own stories; many of the best are collected in *The Nature Of The Catastrophe* (1971), edited by Langdon Jones and Moorcock.

Moorcock's fantasy works include The Dragon In The Sword, Gloriana *(a tribute to* ▷ *Peake and Spenser),* The War Hound And The World's Pain *(in which the Devil attempts his own redemption), and the* End Of Time *series:* An Alien Heat, The Hollow Lands *and* The End Of All Songs. *Sf books include* The Ice Schooner, The Black Corridor, Behold The Man *(an examination of the Christ myth),* The Time Dweller *(collection) and two Jerry Cornelius books,* The Lives And Times Of Jerry Cornelius *(collection) and* The Opium General.

READ·ON
- ● *Mother London*
- ► To Moorcock's fantasy:
  - ▷ Poul Anderson, *The Broken Sword*
  - ▷ Roger Zelazny, *Nine Princes In Amber*
  - ▷ Jack Vance, *The Dying Earth*
- ► To his sf:
  - ▷ Barrington J Bayley, *The Knights Of The Limits*

Michael MOORCOCK • *Stormbringer*

▷ Patricia McKILLIP
THE RIDDLE-MASTER OF HED
(Morgon undertakes a quest to solve the riddle of his own identity)

▷ Poul ANDERSON
THREE HEARTS AND THREE LIONS
(Carlsen is transported from World War 2 to a fantasy world to fight for Law against the dark powers of Chaos)

Cosmic Conflict

▷ Roger ZELAZNY
THE SIGN OF THE UNICORN
(third book of the Amber series, in which the forces of Shadow threaten the strife-torn realm of Amber)

▷ John BRUNNER
THE COMPLEAT TRAVELLER IN BLACK
(moral fables about a mysterious traveller's struggle to bring order out of Chaos)

▷ Doris LESSING
SHIKASTA
(the galactic empires of spiritual Canopus, physical Sirius and criminal Shammat struggle for humanity's soul)

▷ M John HARRISON
VIRICONIUM NIGHTS
(seven aspects of the archetypal city Viriconium, so old that 'the substance of reality no longer quite knows what it ought to be')

George MACDONALD
PHANTASTES
(Anodes stumbles into the world of faery and begins searching for his ideal woman)

▷ Iain BANKS
THE BRIDGE
(the subconscious mind of a car-crash victim explored through his visions of a nightmarish, fantastic bridge)

▷ J G BALLARD
THE CRYSTAL WORLD
*(time crystallises in the West African
jungle, freezing the perceptions of those
within it)*

John BUNYAN
PILGRIM'S PROGRESS
*(the journey from human imperfection to
paradise)*

▷ Robert SHECKLEY
OPTIONS
*(are Tom Mishkin's adventures on the
bizarre planet Harmonia exactly what
they seem?)*

Keri HULME
THE BONE PEOPLE
*(three vivid images of New Zealand,
centred around the upbringing of an
autistic child)*

▷ E R EDDISON
THE MEZENTIAN GATE
*(a king struggles against his own
omnipotence and omniscience)*

▷ Philip K DICK
NOW WAIT FOR LAST YEAR
*(only one man can protect the Earth from
alien depredation – but he's dead. Again.)*

▷ T H WHITE
**THE ONCE AND FUTURE
KING**
*(the King Arthur legend, with Merlin
living backwards in time)*

▷ Kurt VONNEGUT
THE SIRENS OF TITAN
*(Malachi Constant flees to escape his
dreadful fate – but ends up fulfilling it all
too exactly)*

Glen COOK
**A SHADOW OF ALL NIGHT
FALLING**
*(a wizard and a warrior vie for the heart of
Nepanthe as war looms)*

Colin GREENLAND
DAYBREAK ON A DIFFERENT MOUNTAIN
(a cynical aristocrat and a failed poet become entangled in the prophecy of the return of the city's god)

BRENNU-NJÁLS SAGA
(the life and times of a prescient lawyer in medieval Iceland)

▷ C J CHERRYH
GATE OF IVREL
(Vanye, exiled and shamed, is forced to serve a sorceress out of legend)

▷ Fred SABERHAGEN
THE FIRST BOOK OF SWORDS
(millennia after a war which changed the laws of nature, gods again walk the Earth)

▷ Gene WOLFE
THE BOOK OF THE NEW SUN
(the power of a past messiah, preserved in a mysterious artifact, helps Severian fulfil his destiny)

▷ Stephen DONALDSON
THE SECOND CHRONICLES OF THOMAS COVENANT
(Covenant holds the ultimate power – but he is unable to control it)

▷ Bob SHAW
THE PEACE MACHINE
(an unassuming mathematician discovers a solution for world peace and fights for it against authority)

▷ Barrington J BAYLEY
THE ZEN GUN
(space-operatic heroics centred around the possession of an awe-inspiring wooden weapon)

Devices Of Power

Langdon Jones, *The Eye Of The Lens*
▷ J G Ballard, *The Atrocity Exhibition*

MYTH AND LEGEND
▷ Marion Bradley, *The Mists Of Avalon*
  Steven Brust, *To Reign In Hell*
▷ C J Cherryh, *The Dreamstone*
▷ E R Eddison, *The Worm Ouroboros*
  Paul Hazel, *The Finnbranch*
▷ Robert Holdstock, *Mythago Wood*
▷ Guy Gavriel Kay, *The Summer Tree*
▷ Tanith Lee, *Night's Master*
▷ J R R Tolkien, *The Silmarillion*
▷ Roger Zelazny, *Creatures Of Light And Darkness*

MYTHICAL BEASTS
▷ Poul Anderson, *The Merman's Children*
▷ Peter Beagle, *The Last Unicorn*
▷ Jorge Luis Borges, *The Book Of Imaginary Beings*
▷ Barbara Hambly, *Dragonsbane*
  Richard Matheson, *I Am Legend*
▷ Anne McCaffrey, *Dragonflight*
▷ Patricia McKillip, *The Forgotten Beasts Of Eld*
▷ Jack Vance, *The Dragon Masters*
  Jack Williamson, *Darker Than You Think*

N

NEBULA AWARD WINNERS
The Nebula Awards are made annually by the Science Fiction Writers of America (an organisation which, despite its name, admits writers of all nationalities). Like the Hugos, awards are made in a number of categories, but we have only listed the winning novels.

1965: ▷ Frank Herbert, *Dune*
1966: ▷ Daniel Keyes, *Flowers For Algernon* and ▷ Samuel R Delany, *Babel-17* (tie)
1967: ▷ Samuel R Delany, *The Einstein Intersection*

1968: Alexei Panshin, *Rite Of Passage*
1969: ▷ Ursula K LeGuin, *The Left Hand Of Darkness*
1970: ▷ Larry Niven, *Ringworld*
1971: ▷ Robert Silverberg, *A Time Of Changes*
1972: ▷ Isaac Asimov, *The Gods Themselves*
1973: ▷ Arthur C Clarke, *Rendezvous With Rama*
1974: ▷ Ursula K LeGuin, *The Dispossessed*
1975: ▷ Joe Haldeman, *The Forever War*
1976: ▷ Frederik Pohl, *Man Plus*
1977: ▷ Frederik Pohl, *Gateway*
1978: ▷ Vonda N McIntyre, *Dreamsnake*
1979: ▷ Arthur C Clarke, *The Fountains Of Paradise*
1980: ▷ Gregory Benford, *Timescape*
1981: ▷ Gene Wolfe, *The Claw Of The Conciliator*
1982: ▷ Michael Bishop, *No Enemy But Time*
1983: ▷ David Brin, *Startide Rising*
1984: ▷ William Gibson, *Neuromancer*
1985: ▷ Orson Scott Card, *Ender's Game*
1986: ▷ Orson Scott Card, *Speaker For The Dead*
1987: Pat Murphy, *The Falling Woman*

THE NEW WAVE(S)
▷ J G Ballard, *Crash*
▷ Samuel R Delany, *The Einstein Intersection*
▷ Harlan Ellison ed, *Dangerous Visions*
  Langdon Jones and ▷ Michael Moorcock ed, *The Nature Of The Catastrophe*
▷ Michael Moorcock ed, *New Worlds*
▷ John Sladek, *The Reproductive System*
▷ Roger Zelazny, *The Dream Master*

NIVEN, Larry (born 1938)
US novelist and short story writer

Among the most skilled of hard sf writers, Niven writes detailed and inventive evocations of future societies and technologies. His particular specialities are the description of genuinely alien aliens (such as the puppeteers, to whom cowardice is a virtue or the aggressively carnivorous Kzinti), and the examination of how human societies evolve under the pressures of environmental and scientific change (often setting several stories at different periods during the society's evolution). These themes are best explored in the stories set in the Known Space future, describing humanity's gradual expansion into an already heavily populated galaxy. The collection *The Long ARM of Gil Hamilton* (1976) deals with the social traumas caused by organ transplant technology, which gives extended life – provided somebody can be found to provide spare parts. Known Space is also used to examine the social fragmentation caused by slower than light interstellar colonisation, as in *A Gift From Earth* (1968), where the descendants of the ship's crew, who control access to the organ banks, dominate a rigidly hierarchical society. Niven's writing shows his enthusiasm for working out the logical consequences of an idea, no matter how absurd, as in the linked set of humourous fantasy time travel stories *The Flight Of The Horse* (1973).

PROTECTOR (1973)

Protectors are perfectly designed fighting machines, the adult stage of the Pak species, whose adolescent members are not intelligent and exist only to breed. In the novel humans are evolved Breeders, left to fend for themselves when an Earth colony of Pak discovered that an unexpected environmental feature prevented their Breeders from metamorphosing into Protectors. But now the Pak are trying to re-contact their lost colony – and to a Protector, a human is simply a genetically distorted Breeder that must be destroyed to preserve the purity of the race. The biology and psychology of the Pak are ingenious and carefully worked out, as are the details of the fiercely independent society of Asteroid Belt miners who are the first humans in Known Space to contact the Pak.

Niven's other Known Space *books include* World of Ptavvs *and* The Patchwork Girl *and the collections* Neutron Star *and* Tales Of Known Space. *Unconnected books include the collections* All The Myriad Ways, Convergent Series *and* Limits *and the novels* A World Out Of Time *and* The Integral Trees. *He collaborated with* ▷ *Jerry Pournelle on* Lucifer's Hammer, Footfall, Inferno *(playing with theology rather than science),* The Mote In God's Eye *(a somewhat militaristic story of first contact with powerfully described aliens) and* Oath Of Fealty *(urban feudalism).*

READ·ON

● *The Magic Goes Away* applies Niven's hard sf ingenuity to fantasy, in a world where magic is fuelled by mana (a non-renewable resource), and the bones of a continent-sized worm (killed by the mana crisis) become a mountain range

Ringworld and its sequel *The Ringworld Engineers* deal with attempts by a variety of beings from Known Space to explore the vast star-girdling construct of the title

▶ To *Ringworld*:
  ▷ Frederik Pohl, *Gateway*
  ▷ Terry Pratchett, *Strata*

▶ To *The Long ARM of Gil Hamilton*:

▷ Isaac Asimov, *The Caves Of Steel*
► To the aliens:
▷ Frank Herbert, *Whipping Star*
▷ Poul Anderson, *Trader To The Stars*
► ▷ Arthur C Clarke, *Imperial Earth*
▷ John Varley, *The Ophiuchi Hotline*
▷ Ben Bova, *As On A Darkling Plain*
▷ Joe Haldeman, *Mindbridge*

NORMAN, John (born 1931)
US novelist

Norman's seminal work is *The Chronicles Of The Counter-Earth*, an open-ended series set on the Earth's twin planet, Gor. The early books of the series are straightforward adventure novels, but later books become engorged with his theories on the true role of women, namely that they can find true happiness only as degraded slaves. This rampant obsession tends to obscure the virtues of his writing.

READ•ON ► ▷ Edgar Rice Burroughs and
▷ Robert E Howard also wrote extended series of adventure novels in settings broadly resembling Norman's. An alternative view of male/female relationships is offered in
▷ Joanna Russ, *The Female Man*

NORTON, Andre (born 1912)
US novelist

The majority of Norton's novels, such as *The Zero Stone* (1968), are entertaining space operas, intended for teenagers and mostly set in a vaguely defined future including faster-than-light travel, many intelligent alien species and such groups as the Free Traders (galactic tramp merchant ships). Her writing emphasises integration with nature over excessive mechanisation, particularly in such novels as *Catseye* (1961) which involve empathy between humans and intelligent animals. Much of her other writing, such as *The Crystal Gryphon* (1972), is part of the Witch World series, adult fantasies set in a mysterious, magical world, with a strong element of romance.

READ•ON ► To Witch World:
▷ Anne McCaffrey, *The White Dragon*
► To the sf:
Sylvia Engdahl, *Enchantress From The Stars*

O

ORWELL, George (Eric Arthur Blair) (1903–50)
British author and journalist

One of the great social critics of the second quarter of the century, Orwell spoke out in works such as *The Road To Wigan Pier* (1937) against the transcendent misery of everyday life for the poor. His speculative writing betrays a similar concern. A committed humanist and socialist, Orwell opposed totalitarianism in whatever form it took, as is shown in his two best-known novels. *Animal Farm* (1945) bitterly satirises the betrayal of the people's revolution in the USSR, while *1984* (1949) demonstrates chillingly how absolute government means absolute suppression of will. *1984* is an attack on the present, presented as a vision of the future. Orwell condemns the ever-growing tendency of those in power to exercise authority at the expense of individuals' freedoms. In *1984*, even language serves the state. Newspeak makes treasonable ideas, literally, unthinkable. Winston Smith works at the Ministry of Truth, rewriting the historical record. With his lover Julia he rebels, seeking to create a haven of humanity. He is discovered and tortured by the superbly-drawn O'Brien. Winston must be made to love Big Brother, symbol of the State. The boot of tyranny grinds the face of humanity without hope of reprieve.

READ·ON

● *Animal Farm* is a close and savage political satire. A group of farm animals, overthrowing their human masters, find that while all animals are in theory equal, 'some are more equal than others'.

► ▷ Aldous Huxley, *Brave New World,*
▷ Ray Bradbury, *Fahrenheit 451* and
▷ Anthony Burgess, *A Clockwork Orange* each present different, but equally disturbing dystopias. Burgess also wrote *1985*, a right-wing riposte to *1984*.

P

PEAKE, Mervyn (1911–68)
British novelist, short story writer, poet, playwright and artist

Peake was a genius of the bizarre, an admirer of ▷ Poe and ▷ Kafka who drew and wrote with a unique, intense style and texture. His brilliance was only really realised after his death; he made his living teaching and illustrating other people's books. His lightest work is *Mr Pye* (1953), a quirky story set on the island of Sark, describing a modern missionary tormented by unusual material manifestations connected with his spiritual activities: he gradually acquires the wings of an angel. Peake's account of the terrible consequences of saintliness beyond the call of duty – and the equally drastic consequences of Mr Pye's attempts to balance the equation with some random devilry – is amusing and intriguing, with only a hint of the freakishness and grotesquerie for which he is best remembered.

THE TITUS BOOKS (1946–59)
Titus Groan, Gormenghast and *Titus Alone* were only the beginning of a projected series that was to take Titus, the 77th Earl of Gormenghast, from birth to death. Tragically, however, *Titus Alone* was never finished, and all we have of the fourth volume is a few pages of notes. Nevertheless, the trilogy stands as a complex, vivid work, one of the landmarks of modernist literature. The first two books are set in the crumbling, ritual-bound Castle Gormenghast, and describe the birth and Earling of Titus, and his life up to his departure from the Castle. It is a time of crisis: the dangerous, disrespectful ex-scullion Steerpike has put his mind to gaining power in Gormenghast – to which end he is prepared to kill as well as to persuade and seduce. Peake's deadly irony and allegorical bite, strong as they are, are overshadowed by his characters – exaggerated but complex portraits like the sagging chef Swelter, the tombstone-toothed, cheerful Doctor Prunesquallor and Titus' sulky, sultry sister Fuschia, swathed in red; by his setting – one of the most memorable, haunting worlds in all fantasy literature; and, above all, the endless, meaningless system of ritual, into which the characters are inescapably locked. In the underrated *Titus Alone*, however, the rich, ponderous style of *Titus Groan* and *Gormenghast* is left behind as Titus abandons his realm to explore the world outside. The book has an accelerated, hallucinatory quality, and the sudden variety of settings and characters is bewildering and fascinating. More directly allegorical than the previous two books, it is a worthy if unexpected successor.

Peake's other work includes children's books, poetry and art. The superb anthol-

ogy Peake's Progress *contains a generous selection of poems, plays and draw-ings as well as a radio adaptation of* Mr Pye, *and short stories including 'A Boy In Darkness', a Gormenghast tale apart from the main sequence. Peake's widow Maeve Gilmore's biography* A World Away *illustrates with feeling the complexities of Peake's life, as well as providing insight into the generation of his work.*

R E A D • O N   ▶ ▷ Iain Banks, *Walking On Glass*
　　　　　　　　　▷ M John Harrison, *In Viriconium*
　　　　　　　　　▷ Franz Kafka, *The Castle*
　　　　　　　　　▷ Brian Aldiss, *The Malacia Tapestry*
　　　　　　　　　▷ Stanislaw Lem, *Memoirs Found In A Bathtub*

PIERCY, Marge (born 1936)
US novelist and poet

Woman On The Edge Of Time (1976), one of the major utopian novels of the 1970s, juxtaposes accounts of the heroine's brutally uncaring treatment in a modern asylum with the loving nature of the rural community which is either a delusion or a product of her telepathic ability to communicate with the future. The asylum sections are powerful and moving, while the utopian passages are visionary in that readers tend to find them either remarkably naïve or deeply inspiring.

R E A D • O N   ● *Dance The Eagle To Sleep*
　　　　　　　　　▶ Similar utopias are in:
　　　　　　　　　▷ Ursula K LeGuin, *Always Coming Home*
　　　　　　　　　　 Sally Miller Gearhart, *The Wanderground*
　　　　　　　　　▶ To the asylum sections:
　　　　　　　　　　 Ken Kesey, *One Flew Over The Cuckoo's Nest*
　　　　　　　　　　 Paul Sayer, *The Comforts Of Madness*
　　　　　　　　　◊ Feminism

POE, Edgar Allan (1809–49)
US short story writer, poet and novelist

Although Poe was one of the most influential figures in early US literature, his genius was insufficiently appreciated during his short, unhappy life. Many of his stories (gathered in *Tales Of Mystery And Imagination*), use conventional sf themes and devices: balloon flight to the Moon in 'The Unparalleled Adventure Of One Hans Pfaall', cometary holocaust in 'The Conversation Of Eiros And Charmion', strange Antarctic civilisation in 'Narrative Of Arthur Gordon Pym'. However, these ideas are not usually central to the thrust of the tales, which is to present Poe's view of ordinary existence as a shadow of some more significant reality; this is most clearly expounded in 'Mesmeric Revelation' (1844). Stories deal with the demonstration of this strange truth through mesmerism, through near-death experiences ('A Descent Into The Maelstrom') and most interestingly through committing murder ('The Tell-Tale Heart'). It is in works of this latter type, and in those, such as 'The Fall Of The House Of Usher' (about a family's strange links to its ancestral home) in which the 'arabesque' nature of reality (as Poe called it) are evident throughout, that he has had his most direct influence on such later writers as ▷ Lovecraft and Bloch (who followed him faithfully), or ▷ Ballard and ▷ Ellison, who owe a considerable debt to Poe's pioneering exploration of the psychological dimensions of sf.

READ•ON ▶ ▷ J G Ballard, *The Drowned World*
▷ H P Lovecraft, *The Haunter Of The Dark*
▷ Harlan Ellison, *All The Sounds Of Fear*

POHL, Frederik (born 1919)
US novelist and short story writer

Pohl's ability to interweave sardonic social commentary with convincing scientific extrapolation has produced some of science fiction's best known works. In collaboration with ▷ C M Kornbluth, he produced *The Space Merchants* (1953), the satirical vision of a dystopia controlled by advertising agencies. His early short stories were at their best when commenting on American consumerism; 'The Midas Plague' (set in a world of inverted economics, where only the rich can afford not to be surrounded by luxuries) and 'The Tunnel Under The World' (about a man trapped in an advertising experiment; both stories are in *The Best Of Frederik Pohl*, 1975) are both memorable examples. Twenty-five years later, Pohl was still finding new things to say about the social interactions of mankind. In *Man Plus* (1976), a man is painstakingly remodelled as a cyborg in order to adapt him to live on the surface of Mars. As he loses parts of his original body, the protagonist slowly loses his identity; his emotional upheavals are vividly portrayed. *Jem* (1979) depicts the attempts of the three giant economic power blocs of a future Earth to colonise the planet Jem, which already harbours three forms of indigenous sentient life; the effects of Jem on the various political factions are carefully explored.

GATEWAY (1979)
In Pohl's most memorable novel to date, humanity has discovered Gateway, an asteroid-based launch pad for hundreds of starships built by the long-vanished Heechee. The ships are still in working order, but their preset destinations are unknown; those with the courage to try a journey might

return with Heechee treasures, or they might not return at all. Into this setting steps Robinette Broadhead, an emotionally underdeveloped coward who eventually finds riches, surviving the journey by unwittingly abandoning his lover to a black hole. This story is interwoven with Broadhead's interviews with his psychiatrist, long after he becomes wealthy, in which he finally confronts his feelings of guilt about his girlfriend's fate. Without skirting around the emotional problems of his protagonist, Pohl keeps the plot moving to produce a complex and powerful novel that leaves many unanswered questions in the reader's mind. Some of these questions are resolved in the book's sequels: *Beyond The Blue Event Horizon* (1980), *Heechee Rendezvous* (1984) and *The Annals Of The Heechee* (1987).

Frederik Pohl's other works include The Age Of The Pussyfoot, The Coming Of The Quantum Cats, The Years Of The City *(describing the gradual evolution of New York into a form of urban utopia), and the collections* In The Problem Pit *and* The Gold At The Starbow's End *(the title story is a good example of his recent shorter work, dealing with an interstellar mission launched to a non-existent planet in the hope of stimulating transcendental development in its unknowing crew). With* ▷ C M Kornbluth *he wrote* Gladiator At Law *(legal satire) and* Wolfbane, *while the* Starchild *trilogy and the three juveniles* Undersea Quest, Undersea Fleet *and* Undersea City *were written with Jack Williamson.*

R E A D • O N

▶ To *The Space Merchants*:
   ▷ John Brunner, *Stand On Zanzibar*
   Sam J Lundwall, *2018 AD, or The King Kong Blues*
▶ To *Gateway*:
   ▷ Arthur C Clarke, *Rendezvous With Rama*
   ▷ Bob Shaw, *Orbitsville*
▶ To *Man Plus*:
   ▷ Algis Budrys, *Who?*
▶ To *Jem*:
   ▷ Philip K Dick, *Clans Of The Alphane Moon*
   ▷ C J Cherryh, *Downbelow Station*

POST-APOCALYPSE
▷ J G Ballard, *Hello America*
▷ John Crowley, *Engine Summer*
▷ Philip K Dick, *The Penultimate Truth*
▷ Doris Lessing, *Memoirs Of A Survivor*
▷ Walter Miller, *A Canticle For Leibowitz*
▷ Michael Moorcock, *The Ice Schooner*
   Edgar Pangborn, *Davy*

Neville Shute, *On The Beach*
George R Stewart, *Earth Abides*
▷ John Wyndham, *The Chrysalids*

POURNELLE, Jerry (born 1933)
US novelist and short story writer

Though Pournelle is best-known for his collaborations with ▷ Larry Niven, he has also written much sf and technical non-fiction in his own right. Most of his stories are either strongly militaristic and hierarchical (*A Spaceship For The King*, 1973; *The Mote In God's Eye*, with Niven, features the same society at a later stage of its development) or are dominated by international corporations (*High Justice*, 1977). Highly technological in nature, Pournelle's writing is notable for its political conservatism and support for a military lifestyle, interestingly combined (especially in *High Justice*) with enthusiasm for individual liberty.

R E A D • O N   ▶ ▷ Robert A Heinlein, *The Moon Is A Harsh Mistress*
　　　　　　　　　　▷ Gordon R Dickson, *Dorsai!*
　　　　　　　　　▶ To *High Justice*:
　　　　　　　　　　L Neil Smith, *The Probability Broach*

POWERS, Tim (born 1952)
US novelist

Powers' adventure/thriller fantasies are notable for their settings – unusual corners of real Earth history, vividly described, rather than some idyllic sub-Tolkien fairyland – and their well-drawn characters. His heroes tend to be middle-aged, settling down to a quiet retirement when they are called upon to set off on great adventures and face nameless horrors. Old fashioned magic, complete with alchemy and voodoo ritual, is a constant factor. *The Anubis Gates* (1983) mixes all the elements of Powers' work with a cunningly worked-out time-travel paradox and famous literary figures from nineteenth-century London. The hero's discovery that life in a previous century is not as easy as he had imagined – especially when one is being pursued by a group of sinister black magicians – lends an essential dash of farce. Powers barrels around the convolutions of the plot with dash and verve, and with his larger-than-life heroes and villains he brews up a hugely enjoyable adventure.

R E A D • O N   ● Powers' other historical fantasies are *The Drawing Of The Dark* (King Arthur returns in sixteenth-century Vienna as the Turks invade Europe) and *On Stranger Tides* (an eighteenth-century Caribbean pirate adventure). *Dinner At Deviant's Palace* is straight sf but retains an element of horror.

▶ ▷ K W Jeter, *Infernal Devices*
James P Blaylock, *Homunculus*
▷ George R R Martin, *Fevre Dream*
▷ John Barth, *The Sot-Weed Factor*
Barry Hughart, *Bridge Of Birds*

PRATCHETT, Terry (born 1948)
British novelist

Pratchett's first novel, the children's fantasy *The Carpet People,* was published in 1971, and *Strata,* his inspired parody of ▷ Niven's *Ringworld,* in 1981. His endless supply of bizarre ideas and quirky perspectives crams his work with lively and imaginative humour. Colourful and readable, but far from vacuous, his books contain many well-drawn, memorable characters, while his genius for low comedy is unrivalled in sf. *The Colour Of Magic* (1983), which catapulted him to fame, is the first of the Discworld books, set on a flat world borne through the stellar void on the back of a cosmic turtle. It contains four parodic novellas featuring Twoflower (an excessively rich tourist with animated, ferocious luggage) and the inept wizard Rincewind whom he hires as a guide to help him satisfy his desire to experience the rougher side of Discworld life. Twoflower's wish is soon granted, as there are all too many people only too keen to part him from both his money and his life. Their adventures continue in *The Light Fantastic* (1986), both books should appeal to anyone with a taste for the ridiculous and a tolerance for the occasional dire pun.

READ·ON
● A total of six Discworld books have been published. *Equal Rites* and *Mort* follow *The Light Fantastic*; more considered, but hilarious nonetheless.

▶ ▷ Harry Harrison, *Bill, The Galactic Hero*
David Langford, *The Leaky Establishment*
Craig Shaw Gardner, *A Malady Of Magicks*
Barry Hughart, *Bridge Of Birds*
Tom Holt, *Expecting Someone Taller*

PRIEST, Christopher (born 1943)
British novelist and short story writer

Alienation and altered perceptions are Priest's characteristic themes, appearing in work as early as *Indoctrinaire* (a nightmarish tale of time travel and global war, 1970). His more thoughtful later novels are excellently characterised and lyrical meditations on solipsism and creativity. *A Dream Of Wessex* (1977), for example, is a love story set in a dream future which only exists in the subconscious minds of its participants. The protagonist of *The Affirmation* (1981) redefines both himself and his reality as he writes and rewrites his autobiography. Priest's most recent work, *The Glamour* (1984), plays fascinating games with memory and identity: invisibility becomes a metaphor for alienation, focusing on our failure to remember those we do not wish to know. *Inverted World* (1974) describes a bizarre world whose surface goes to infinity and back again, where time and space behave in a way utterly alien to our experience; humans cannot survive more than a short distance from the constantly moving 'optimum point'. The hero's gradually increasing understanding of the true nature of his world makes this one of the most famous 'idea stories' of sf.

READ·ON

● *An Infinite Summer* (a collection whose themes echo those of the late novels)

▶ To *Inverted World*:
  ▷ Philip K Dick, *Time Out Of Joint*
▶ To the later novels:
  ▷ M John Harrison, *A Storm Of Wings*
  ▷ John Crowley, *Aegypt*
  Christopher Evans, *The Insider*
  Paul Auster, *The New York Trilogy*

PSI POWERS
▷ Alfred Bester, *The Demolished Man*
▷ Marion Zimmer Bradley, *The Heritage Of Hastur*
▷ Julian May, *The Many-Coloured Land*
▷ Anne McCaffrey, *To Ride Pegasus*
  James H Schmitz, *The Witches Of Karres*
▷ Robert Silverberg, *Dying Inside*
▷ Theodore Sturgeon, *More Than Human*
▷ A E van Vogt, *Slan*

PSYCHOLOGY
▷ Gregory Benford, *The Stars In Shroud*
▷ Angela Carter, *The Infernal Desire Machines Of Dr Hoffman*

▷ D G Compton, *Synthajoy*
▷ Philip José Farmer, *Strange Relations*
▷ Robert Silverberg, *The Second Trip*
  Robert Louis Stevenson, *Dr Jekyll And Mr Hyde*
▷ Roger Zelazny, *The Dream Master*

PYNCHON, Thomas (born 1937)
US novelist and short story writer

The use of sf themes and approaches characterises Pynchon's work and, like ▷ Kafka, he has influenced many genre writers. His interests include paranoid world views, the nature of authoritarian societies and the terror of entropy, all presented in a blackly humorous fashion. *The Crying Of Lot 49* (1966) is a conspiracy theory book which explores contrasting views of reality as predetermined machine and reality as full of secret meaning. *Gravity's Rainbow* (1973) is concerned with all of the above themes and told in a dense, allusive prose resembling that of James Joyce.

READ·ON   ● *V*
            ▶ Robert Shea and
            ▷ Robert Anton Wilson, *Illuminatus!*
            ▷ Kurt Vonnegut, *Cat's Cradle*
              G K Chesterton, *The Man Who Was Thursday*
              Joseph Heller, *Catch-22*

R

RELIGION
▷ James Blish, *A Case Of Conscience*
▷ Richard Cowper, *The Road To Corlay*
▷ Philip K Dick, *A Maze Of Death*
▷ Robert A Heinlein, *Stranger In A Strange Land*
▷ Frank Herbert, *Dune*
▷ Barry Malzberg, *The Cross Of Fire*
▷ Walter M Miller, *A Canticle For Leibowitz*
▷ Olaf Stapledon, *Star Maker*
▷ Roger Zelazny, *Lord Of Light*

RICE, Anne
British novelist

Rice's brilliant, believable evocation of vampiric life encourages empathy with creatures often reluctant to accept their own nature. Her two major characters-cum-narrators – Louis in *Interview With The Vampire* (1976), his mentor in *The Vampire Lestat* (1986) – are not the remote, terrifying and clichéd monsters of myth. The 'autobiographical' format shows the vampires, their society, and the larger world with meticulous detail and superb characterisation. Lestat and Louis are iconoclasts who discover the true limits to their abilities and history against a complementary background of general history.

R E A D • O N　　▶ ▷ Fred Saberhagen, *The Dracula Tape*
　　　　　　　　　　　　Chelsea Quinn Yarbro, *Hotel Transylvania*

ROBERTS, Keith (born 1935)
British novelist, short story writer and illustrator

Roberts' penchant for pastoral settings and low (often steam powered) technology is epitomised in *Pavane* (1968), set in a Britain where the Reformation never happened and science is savagely suppressed by the Catholic Church. In *The Chalk Giants* (1974), the survivors of a nuclear war revert to a primitive way of life and the worship of a grain god. *Molly Zero* (1980), by contrast, describes Molly's escape from the Blocks in a near-future Britain under martial law. The excellent collection *Ladies From Hell* (1979) includes 'Our Lady Of Desperation', about an artist in a bureaucratic near-future where all such 'social undesirables' are subject to personal overseers. *Kiteworld* (1985) is, like many of Roberts' books, a 'fix-up' of short stories. Set in the post-holocaust Realm, where great kites are flown day and night to prevent the coming of the Demons of the Badlands (the distant memories of nuclear missiles), the book follows the lives of many characters as the Variant and Middle Doctrine churches vie for control. Despite the book's slightly flawed deus ex machina ending, Roberts' feeling for his settings and characters ensure that the reader is not disappointed.

R E A D • O N　　● 　*Kaeti And Company* (about the tough, streetwise Kaeti)
　　　　　　　　　　　　The Inner Wheel
　　　　　　　　　　　　Gráinne (Celtic myth-figure as media priestess)
　　　　　　　　　　　　The Grain Kings (collection)
　　　　　　　　　▶ ▷ Brian Aldiss, *Greybeard*
　　　　　　　　　　　　Kingsley Amis, *The Alteration*

▷ Richard Cowper, *The Road To Corlay*
Edgar Pangborn, *Davy*

ROBINSON, Kim Stanley (born 1952)
US novelist and short story writer

One of the most prominent of the new generation of American authors, Robinson has produced a number of unusually ingenious novels. *Icehenge* (1985) explores the relation of history to human memory in its story of an inexplicable monument discovered on the surface of Pluto, while *The Memory Of Whiteness* (1987) describes the unification of a new form of deterministic physics with music and philosophy. Many of Robinson's short stories are also highly regarded, particularly the award-winning fantasies 'Stone Eggs' and 'Black Air' (in *The Planet On The Table*, 1986).

READ·ON

● *The Wild Shore*
▶ To *Icehenge*:
  Hilbert Schenk, *A Rose For Armageddon*
▶ To *The Memory Of Whiteness*:
  Charles Harness, *The Rose*
▷ Stanislaw Lem, *The Investigation*

ROBOTS
▷ Isaac Asimov, *The Complete Robot*
▷ Barrington J Bayley, *The Soul Of The Robot*
▷ Philip K Dick, *Do Androids Dream Of Electric Sheep?*
▷ Stanislaw Lem, *The Cyberiad*
▷ Rudy Rucker, *Software*
▷ Clifford Simak, *City*
▷ John Sladek, *The Reproductive System*
Jack Williamson, *The Humanoids*

RUCKER, Rudy
US writer of novels, short stories and non-fiction

Rucker is fascinated by the bizarre philosophical implications of mathematical logic, a theme he brings to life in *Software*, which investigates the differences between artificial and natural intelligences, and the celebration of transfinite number theory *White Light*. The narrator, visiting Heaven, encounters an infinitely high (and infinitely distant) mountain analogous to the sequence of infinite numbers, a library where he is forced to deposit all of his possible autobiographies, and a climax which offers the provocative if quirky insight that zero and infinity are the same thing.

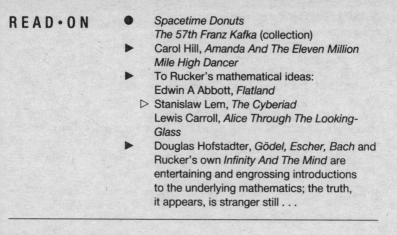

READ·ON

● Spacetime Donuts
   The 57th Franz Kafka (collection)

▶ Carol Hill, Amanda And The Eleven Million
   Mile High Dancer

▶ To Rucker's mathematical ideas:
   Edwin A Abbott, Flatland

▷ Stanislaw Lem, The Cyberiad
   Lewis Carroll, Alice Through The Looking-
   Glass

▶ Douglas Hofstadter, Gödel, Escher, Bach and
   Rucker's own Infinity And The Mind are
   entertaining and engrossing introductions
   to the underlying mathematics; the truth,
   it appears, is stranger still . . .

RUSS, Joanna (born 1937)
US novelist and short story writer

Many of Russ' stories depend on the framework of the genre's shared ideas
while questioning their assumptions. Her reassessments are often feminist
in intent, as in *The Two Of Them* (1978), a pessimistic story of the conflict
between a woman and her male superior, triggered by her rescue of a girl
from a society where women are kept in harems, and *The Adventures Of
Alyx* (1976, featuring a tough, competent female hero). *We Who Are About
To . . .* (1977) examines instead the ridiculously over-optimistic colonisation
efforts of survivors from a wrecked spaceship, seen through the eyes of a
woman who wants only to die. *The Female Man* (1975) brings together four
women from contrasted alternate Earths: our own world, a close copy where
male-female relations resemble ours of the 1940s, a reality where all the men
are long dead and an Earth where the battle between the sexes has become
a shooting war. The book's strongest feature is probably its vicious, accurate
and funny observation of the way men and women play out their roles, while
the fragmentary, experimental style adds to the book's impact as one of the
most comprehensive and witty sf expressions of the female experience.

READ·ON

● And Chaos Died (a novel which captures the
   true strangeness of mind to mind contact)
   Extra(Ordinary) People (collection, including
   the award-winning novella 'Souls')

▶ ▷ Josephine Saxton, The Power Of Time
   Zoë Fairbairns, Benefits

▶ To We Who Are About To . . .:
   Charles Logan, Shipwreck

◊ Feminism

RUSSELL, Eric Frank (1905–78)
British novelist and short story writer   '

Russell favoured a witty, fast-moving style, effectively deployed in novels like *Three To Conquer* (1956), in which intelligent parasites from Venus invade Earth. His humans usually triumph over aliens, as in *Wasp* (1957), the entertaining story of a lone spy conquering a planet, but he frequently adds a touch of paranoia (eg in *Sinister Barrier,* 1948). Many of his short stories are satirical, as in 'Allamagoosa' (about bureaucratic ignorance and inflexibility, included in *Far Stars,* 1961) or '. . . And Then There Were None' (in *The Great Explosion,* 1962), in which a society of pacifist anarchists defeats the crew of a military spaceship.

R E A D • O N   ▶   To *Sinister Barrier*:
                          ▷ Robert A Heinlein, *The Puppet Masters*
                      ▶   To *Wasp*:
                          ▷ Harry Harrison, *The Stainless Steel Rat*

RYMAN, Geoff
British novelist and short story writer

In such stories as *The Unconquered Country* (1987), a short novel which chronicles the destruction of a future 'Third World' nation, Ryman shows a depth of understanding of his themes and characters that is rare in sf. *The Warrior Who Carried Life* (1985) is one of the most intellectually stimulating fantasies of recent years, brilliantly integrating elements of philosophy and romance with the epic of Gilgamesh and a feminist interpretation of Genesis.

R E A D • O N   ▶ ▷ Samuel R Delany, *Stars In My Pocket Like Grains Of Sand*
                          ▷ John Crowley, *Engine Summer*
                      ▶   The short stories of
                          ▷ James Tiptree

S

SABERHAGEN, Fred (born 1930)
US novelist and short story writer

Saberhagen's readable, entertaining books range from the hard sf of the

Berserker series (eg *The Berserker Wars* (stories), 1981; *Berserker's Planet,* 1975) through the science fantasy of *Empire Of The East* (1979) to the fantasy of the Dracula and Swords books. The Berserker series depicts the ultimate Doomsday weapon of an ancient race – self-reproducing war machines with the mission of destroying all life. Humanity's struggle against this archetypal enemy is used to throw more usual human problems into sharp relief.

READ·ON ● *The Dracula Tape* (a sympathetic retelling of the Dracula myth)
The First Book Of Swords
▶ ▷ Roger Zelazny, *The Last Defender Of Camelot*
Randall Garrett, *Too Many Magicians*

SATIRE
Ron Goulart, *The Sword Swallower*
▷ Frederik Pohl and ▷ C M Kornbluth, *The Space Merchants*
▷ Doris Lessing, *The Sentimental Agents In The Volyen Empire*
▷ Robert Sheckley, *Journey Beyond Tomorrow*
Jonathan Swift, *Gulliver's Travels*
William Tenn, *Of All Possible Worlds*
Mark Twain, *A Connecticut Yankee In King Arthur's Court*

SAXTON, Josephine (born 1935)
British novelist and short story writer

Queen of the States (1986) is a surreal, engrossing study of the supposed mental illness of Magdalen Hayward. Saxton gleefully blurs the boundaries between reality and Magdalen's fantasies, and explores the rubble-strewn landscapes of sex, dreaming and drugs with ▷ Dickian zest. Her other work, including *The Hieros Gamos Of Sam And An Smith, Vector For Seven* and *Group Feast,* tackles similar themes with an emphasis on some form of spiritual progress. Collections are *The Power Of Time* (1985) and *The Travails Of Jane Saint And Other Stories* (1980).

READ·ON ▶ ▷ Philip K Dick, *A Scanner Darkly*
▷ Angela Carter, *The Infernal Desire Machines Of Dr Hoffman*
▶ To the short stories:
▷ J G Ballard, *The Terminal Beach*
◊ Feminism

SCIENCE
(the ethics, philosophy and methodology of science – and scientists)

▷ Gregory Benford, *Timescape*
▷ D G Compton, *The Electric Crocodile*
Charles Harness, *The Rose*
▷ Stanislaw Lem, *The Investigation*
▷ Kim Stanley Robinson, *The Memory Of Whiteness*
▷ Norman Spinrad, *Songs From The Stars*
▷ Arkady and Boris Strugatsky, *The Snail On The Slope*

SCIENCE AND SORCERY
▷ Poul Anderson, *Operation Chaos*
▷ Marion Zimmer Bradley, *Stormqueen!*
David Gerrold and ▷ Larry Niven, *The Flying Sorcerors*
▷ Fritz Leiber, *Gather, Darkness!*
▷ Michael Moorcock, *The Jewel In The Skull*
▷ Andre Norton, *Witch World*
▷ Fred Saberhagen, *Empire Of The East*
Christopher Stasheff, *The Warlock In Spite Of Himself*
▷ Jack Vance, *The Dying Earth*
▷ Roger Zelazny, *Lord Of Light*

SEX AND SEXUALITY
Kathy Acker, *Empire Of The Senseless*
▷ J G Ballard, *Crash*
Michael Blumlein, *The Movement Of Mountains*
▷ Angela Carter, *The Infernal Desire Machines Of Dr Hoffman*
▷ Philip José Farmer, *The Lovers*
▷ K W Jeter, *Dr Adder*
▷ Ursula K LeGuin, *The Left Hand Of Darkness*
▷ Naomi Mitchison, *Solution Three*
▷ Michael Moorcock, *The Brothel In Rosenstrasse*
▷ Theodore Sturgeon, *Venus Plus X*

SHAW, Bob (born 1931)
Irish novelist and short story writer

Shaw's main literary interest is in the human ramifications of unusual science. Although the science sparks his stories, and fuels them with problems of ethics or illuminates them with beautiful, poetic images, they are equally devoted to their characters. *Other Days, Other Eyes* (1972) considers a multitude of uses for 'slow glass' (a glass which light takes a great deal of time to penetrate), many of them essentially metaphors for the ways our present lives are haunted by the past, and demonstrates Shaw's gift for the depiction of tragic relationships. Other ingenious pieces of physics include *A Wreath Of*

Stars' anti-neutrino planet, *Orbitsville*'s star-enclosing Dyson sphere and *The Two-Timers*'s alternate time tracks. *The Ragged Astronauts* (1986) varies from Shaw's usual work by being set in a detailed low-technology society (rather than a contemporary or near-future Earth), which exists on a planet whose moon is of similar size and shares its atmosphere. Threatened by deadly airborne mutations, the inhabitants are forced to emigrate to the moon by balloon. Unusually strong characterisation complements the usual scientific interest, and particularly welcome is Shaw's diversification into such fields as biology. The story is continued in *The Wooden Spaceships* (1988) and a third novel is promised.

READ·ON
- ● *Cosmic Kaleidoscope* (collection)
- ▶ David Masson, *The Caltraps Of Time*
- ▶ Peculiar planetary systems:
  - ▷ Larry Niven, *Ringworld*
  - ▷ Brian Aldiss, *Helliconia Spring*
  - ▷ Christopher Priest, *Inverted World*

SHECKLEY, Robert (born 1928)
US novelist and short story writer

Sheckley is one of science fiction's greatest and best-known satirists. Although he is regarded as a master of the short story, and his collections are highly enjoyable, his novels offer deeper pleasures without losing satirical edge. *Dimension Of Miracles* (1968) is typical. Thomas Carmody, an unremarkable Earthling, accidentally wins a prize in the Galactic Lottery and is whisked to the galactic centre to receive it. Unfortunately, he is then left with the problem of getting home . . . What follows is a series of brilliant episodes, in which Carmody meets, among others, a god trying to find a purpose in life, the man who built the planet Earth, and a sentient city. *Journey Beyond Tomorrow* (1962), a rambling trip through a near-future America, is similarly episodic, but is more overtly satirical. *The Status Civilisation* (1960), however, avoids this construction. It deals with Will Barrent's life on the status-obsessed prison planet Omega, which inverts Earth society, and with his subsequent escape back to Earth, which turns out to be the utopia to reflect Omega's dystopia. This novel is not only a satire but a psychological metaphor, and above all a hugely entertaining read.

OPTIONS (1977)
Sheckley's most complex, bizarre and provocative novel begins innocently enough, with interstellar postman Tom Mishkin being forced to land on the planet Harmonia for a spare part. After this the author pretends to find himself in difficulties, slipping characters and ideas in and out of the story at random, apologising to his hero for the mess he's landed him in,

and frequently appearing himself in desperate bids to bring Mishkin and the spare part together and so wrap up the plot. Meanwhile, Mishkin is busy encountering imaginary castles, interrupting games of poker conducted on planks over ravines, chopping down bill collectors disguised as trees, confronting his own negative infatuation with oranges . . . What is going on? An hallucination? A boyish game? A breakdown of causality? A tour of Mishkin's subconscious? A Zen text? The facts are clear; they're down in the book. The options of the title are the numerous optional interpretations.

Other sf novels include Mindswap *(a* Dimension Of Miracles-*type romp),* Tenth Victim *(filmed as La Decima Vittima),* Dramocles, Victim Prime *and* The Alchemical Marriage Of Alistair Crompton, *about a man trying to reunite the divided aspects of his personality. The collection* The Robert Sheckley Omnibus *includes the novella* Immortality, Inc.

READ • ON

- ● *The People Trap* (collection)
- ▶ Italo Calvino, *Cosmicomics*
  Ron Goulart, *After Things Fell Apart*
  - ▷ Stanislaw Lem, *The Futurological Congress*
  - ▷ John Sladek, *Keep The Giraffe Burning*
    Howard Waldrop, *All About Strange Monsters Of The Recent Past*
- ▶ The early satires follow in the footsteps of Swift, *Gulliver's Travels*
  Voltaire, *Candide*
- ▶ From *The Status Civilisation*:
  - ▷ Alfred Bester, *The Demolished Man*
- ▶ From *Options*:
  Tom Stoppard, *The Real Inspector Hound*
  - ▷ Robert Anton Wilson, *Schrödinger's Cat* offers another set of 'options'
    Laurence Sterne, *Tristram Shandy* is the life-inside-a-novel novel to end them all

---

SHEFFIELD, Charles (born 1935)
British/US novelist and short story writer

One of the more imaginative practitioners of the tradition begun by ▷ Verne, Sheffield concentrates on the exposition of scientific ideas and the evocation of a 'sense of wonder'. His books include *The Web Between The Worlds* (1979), describing the construction of a 'space elevator' from the Earth's surface to geostationary orbit and *Sight Of Proteus* (1978), about humans who can wear vat-grown bodies of almost any shape. The impressive *Between The Strokes*

Of Night (1985) deals partly with a near-future Earth approaching nuclear holocaust and partly with a far future contact between star travellers and an apparently alien race.

READ·ON
- ●   *Vectors* (collection)
- ▶ ▷   James Blish, *Cities In Flight*
-    ▷   Robert L Forward, *Dragon's Egg*
-    ▷   Greg Bear, *Eon*

SHELLEY, Mary (1797–1851)
British novelist

In *Frankenstein: or, The Modern Prometheus* (1818), Shelley created what is probably sf/horror's best-known character: the pitiful monster, cobbled together from human remains and galvanised into life during a thunderstorm. Shelley's plot – rarely followed on screen – has the monster, soured by its creator's revulsion, kill his wife and brother during a destructive rampage. The novel ends as Frankenstein perishes in vengeful pursuit of his creation. *Frankenstein*, while set firmly in the Gothic tradition, is often seen as the first true sf work, investigating the results of tampering with forces beyond human ken.

READ·ON
- ●   Shelley's other sf novel, *The Last Man*, is notable for originating the device of the plague which leaves a sole human survivor.
- ▶ ▷   Ursula K LeGuin, *A Wizard Of Earthsea*
-    ▷   Karel Capek, *R.U.R.*
-    ▷   James Blish, *Doctor Mirabilis*

SHEPARD, Lucius (born 1948)
US novelist and short story writer

Shepard's work explores contemporary issues with passion, fusing speculative science and the supernatural in such pieces as the novel *Green Eyes* (a mingling of technological resurrection and voodoo mysteries, 1986) or 'A Spanish Lesson' (involving a nightmarishly vivid picture of a mythically exaggerated Third Reich; in the collection *The Jaguar Hunter*, 1987). Shepard's fascination with blood and magic peaks in his stories of a near-future Central American war; the heart of the sequence is *Life During Wartime* (1988), a haunting novel of soldiers whose brutal high technology environment has become paradoxically full of poetry and myth.

READ·ON   ●   *The Scalehunter's Beautiful Daughter*
            ▶ ▷ Harlan Ellison, *Deathbird Stories*
                Gabriel García Márquez, *One Hundred Years Of Solitude*

SILVERBERG, Robert (born 1936)
US writer of novels, short stories and non-fiction

After writing a large number of pulp sf adventure stories, Silverberg had an amazing burst of creativity in the late 1960s and early 1970s. These later works are well-written and excellent: full of powerfully drawn characters and exciting ideas, integrated with themes of considerable power and beauty. The idea of immortality is central to many of them, through mystic practices in the ingeniously structured and deeply moving contemporary fantasy *The Book Of Skulls* (1972) or by scientific resurrection in the brilliantly unsettling 'Born With The Dead' (in the 1974 collection *Born With The Dead*). Another recurrent theme is the experience of telepathic and emotional communion, presented as a quasi-religious ecstasy in such novels as *A Time Of Changes* (1971, about a society whose religion of self-reliance has crippled its members' ability to love). A long gap followed; but recently Silverberg has resumed writing with such entertaining (if rather less thoughtful) novels as *Lord Valentine's Castle* (1980), the first of a trilogy set on the colourful and diverse world of Majipoor.

DYING INSIDE (1972)
Here Silverberg movingly inverts his theme of fulfilment through telepathic communion. The protagonist, David Selig, is a native of present day New York City who is both blessed and cursed with the power to read minds – a power that is slowly fading. During the course of the novel Selig tells us how the power has provided him with many moments of lonely ecstasy, but in the process has ruined all the conventional hopes of his life. Nevertheless, at the end of the book Selig, shorn of his ability, achieves a kind of peace.

Silverberg's other novels include The Man In The Maze, Hawksbill Station, Son Of Man, The World Inside *(describing from many viewpoints life on a massively overpopulated future Earth)*, Gilgamesh The King *(historical fantasy)*, Shadrach In The Furnace, Nightwings, The Stochastic Man, The Second Trip *(a powerful dramatisation of the problems of a divided self)*, Downward To The Earth *(a story of the post-colonial experience on an alien world) and the more recent* Tom O'Bedlam *and* Star Of Gypsies. *His short story collections include* The Feast Of St Dionysus, Unfamiliar Territory *and* The Conglomeroid Cocktail Party.

READ·ON   ●   *Thorns* (which explores the inextricable links

between our perception of being alive and our
ability to suffer pain)
Tower Of Glass (the interwoven stories of a
man's obsession with alien contact and of his
uncertain relationship with the race of human
beings he creates as slaves)
To *Lord Valentine's Castle*:
The Majipoor Chronicles (collection)
Valentine Pontifex
► To *Dying Inside*:
▷ Joanna Russ, *And Chaos Died*
Leigh Kennedy, *The Journal Of Nicholas The
American*
► To the theme of telepathic communion:
▷ Theodore Sturgeon, *More Than Human*
▷ James Tiptree, *Up The Walls Of The World*
◊ *Immortals*

SIMAK, Clifford (1904–88)
US novelist and short story writer

Although Simak dealt with a wide range of themes, his books all share a similar
pastoral perspective and American small-town sense of values. This can be
seen particularly in his most famous book, *City* (1952), a story of the robots
and intelligent dogs who inherit the Earth after most of humanity emigrates
to the surface of Jupiter. Simak's writing often involves the solution of a multi-
layered enigma, as in *Ring Around The Sun* (1953) and *The Werewolf Principle* (1967), which opens with the protagonist found in space in suspended
animation, amnesiac but able to change into alien forms, and continues with
his discovery of his nature and the purpose of his existence. *Way Station*
(1963) is an American house which serves as a stopping-off point for alien
star travellers, guarded by a man who (with the help of alien medicine) has
lived since the Civil War. The station keeper has over the years absorbed
many alien values and, in a conflict typical of Simak's work, must eventually
make a choice between humanity and the stars.

READ·ON
● *Why Call Them Back From Heaven?* (about
the possibilities of immortality)
Special Deliverance (an entertaining alternate
worlds story)
All The Traps Of Earth (collection)
Shakespeare's Planet
► To *The Werewolf Principle*:
▷ Philip K Dick, *A Scanner Darkly*

SLADEK, John (born 1937)
US novelist and short story writer

Sladek is one of the most prominent writers of satirical sf, with a strong sense of morality beneath his work's manic surface. His novels are full of fascinating and original ideas, often concerned with the philosophy or nature of computer intelligences. These provide a lens through which to view the human race in such books as *Tik-Tok* (1983), the story of how a psychotic but charismatic robot becomes President of the USA, or *The Müller-Fokker Effect* (1970), in which a man encoded onto computer tape is fought over by a variety of bizarre people who want him/it for their own purposes. *Keep The Giraffe Burning* (1977) and *The Lunatics of Terra* (1984) contain surreal short stories, strongly reminiscent of the work of ▷ Robert Sheckley. *Roderick* (1980) is the story of a young robot designed to learn, brought up as a 'real' boy and trying to come to terms with the human race and their attitudes towards him. The robot hero is the most sympathetic of a hilarious collection of personalities (including two touchingly portrayed, aging sf writers, transsexuals, who become Roderick's only true friends).

READ · ON ● *The Reproductive System* (about self-replicating machines which get out of control)
The Steam-Driven Boy (short stories and some excellent sf parodies)
Roderick At Random (the sequel to *Roderick*)
► ▷ Robert Sheckley, *Dimension Of Miracles*
  ▷ Kurt Vonnegut, *Cat's Cradle*

SMITH, Cordwainer (1913–66)
US novelist and short story writer

Smith's unusual and elegant fiction was heavily influenced by classical Chinese narrative techniques. Often employing mythic themes, he wrote in a strongly lyrical style, making considerable use of rhymes and poetic rhythm. Most of his work is set in the common future of the 'Instrumentality' and is full of marvellous inventions, from the telepathic fighting cats, duelling mentally with enemies who exist only in hyperspace, of 'The Game Of Rat And Dragon', to the half-dead, half-alive spacemen of 'Scanners Live In Vain' (both in *The Rediscovery Of Man*. His stories examine authority, religion and free will through conflicts spanning millennia of future history – whose conclusion, tragically, he did not live to write. *Norstrilia* (1975) is Smith's only sf novel, the richly plotted odyssey of Rod McBan, who with the help of an ancient computer manipulates his holding of the immortality drug, stroon, to gain legal ownership of Earth itself. McBan's story is woven of many strands, but particularly of his love for C'mell (a human-like 'underperson' bred as a slave from cat stock) and his involvement in the underpeople's struggle for religious and personal freedom.

READ·ON
- *Quest Of The Three Worlds* (collection) *The Instrumentality Of Mankind* mixes Instrumentality material with stories on other subjects
- ▶ Michael Coney, *The Celestial Steam Locomotive*
- ▶ In theme (if not flavour):
- ▷ Doris Lessing, *Shikasta*

SMITH, E(dward) E(lmer) 'Doc' (1890–1965)
US novelist

Smith's novels are the quintessence of old-style space opera, in which inhumanly virtuous men guard beautiful women from unrelenting evil, against a backdrop of planet-sized spaceships and galaxy-spanning empires. His stories are imaginative, full of unusual (if scientifically unlikely) ideas and plotted on a scale that few other writers have even attempted. The Skylark series (starting with *The Skylark of Space,* 1946) describes the adventures of inventor Richard Seaton, who accidentally discovers a space drive and soon zooms off into the void along with various companions and enemies. Each book expands the scale of the action, from the interplanetary war of the first to the universe-encompassing threats of the last. The Lensman series, beginning with *Triplanetary* (1950), describes a millennia-old war between a good cosmic race, the Arisians, and an evil cosmic race, the Eddorians. Both sides employ lesser beings as soldiers, and the climax of the series is the last battle between the Eddorians and a group of humans bred by the Arisians to succeed themselves as galactic guardians.

READ·ON
- *Spacehounds of IPC*
- ▶ The Lensman series has an official continuation in David Kyle, *Dragon Lensman*
- ▶ ▷ A E Van Vogt, *The Voyage Of The Space Beagle*
  Jack Williamson, *Seetee Ship*
- ▷ Harry Harrison, *Star Smashers Of The Galaxy Rangers* is a parody
- ◊ Space Opera

SORCERORS

Lynn Abbey, *Daughter Of The Bright Flame*
▷ John Brunner, *The Compleat Traveller In Black*
Jo Clayton, *Moongather*
Glen Cook, *A Shadow Of All Night Falling*
▷ Lord Dunsany, *The Charwoman's Shadow*
▷ Tanith Lee, *Volkhavaar*
Megan Lindholm, *Wizard Of The Pigeons*
▷ Patricia McKillip, *The Riddle-Master Of Hed*
▷ Michael Moorcock, *Stormbringer*
▷ Jack Vance, *Rhialto The Marvellous*

SPACE OPERA

▷ Poul Anderson, *Ensign Flandry*
▷ Iain M Banks, *Consider Phlebas*
▷ Barrington J Bayley, *Star Virus*
Suzette Haden Elgin, *Star-Anchored, Star-Angered*
Edmond Hamilton, *The Weapon From Beyond*
▷ Harry Harrison, *Star Smashers Of The Galaxy Rangers*
▷ George R R Martin, *Dying Of The Light*
▷ E E 'Doc' Smith, *First Lensman*
▷ Jack Vance, *The Star King*

SPACESHIPS

▷ Brian Aldiss, *Non-Stop*
▷ Poul Anderson, *Tau Zero*
▷ Barrington J Bayley, *Star Winds*
▷ Robert L Forward, *The Flight Of The Dragonfly*
▷ Robert Heinlein, *Orphans Of The Sky*
▷ Anne McCaffrey, *The Ship Who Sang*
▷ Bob Shaw, *The Wooden Spaceships*
▷ Norman Spinrad, *The Void Captain's Tale*

SPINRAD, Norman (born 1940)
US novelist and short story writer

Spinrad achieved early notoriety for *Bug Jack Barron* (1969), which deals with the corruption of a near-future US, explored through the moral choices forced upon Jack Barron, a populist TV personality. A similar fascination with power relationships is shown in all of Spinrad's early novels; *Agent Of Chaos* (1967) studies the true wielders of influence in a regimented society, while *The Men In The Jungle* (1967) examines the demands of commitment. Spinrad is also a significant writer of short stories, most notable for his studies of perception; a good example is 'All The Sounds Of The Rainbow', in *No Direction Home* (1975). Spinrad's later work is more controlled – at least in style. *The Void Captain's Tale* (1983), for example, describes the protagonist's sexual relationship with his 'Void Pilot', the woman whose orgasms guide their ship through hyperspace. The Captain becomes obsessed with the transcendent orgasmic pleasure only his Pilot can feel, and agrees to help her pass on to a higher state of being by making a random hyperspatial jump and thus dooming his ship. Set in the same universe, *Child Of Fortune* (1985) describes the passage of its heroine into adulthood, as she explores the range of experiences her civilisation has to offer.

READ·ON

● *The Iron Dream* (the heroic fantasy novel Hitler might have written)
Songs From The Stars (an investigation of ends justifying means via the post-holocaust rediscovery of 'evil' technology)
The Last Hurrah Of The Golden Horde (collection)

▶ To the early novels:
Bradley Denton, *Wrack And Roll*

▶ To *The Void Captain's Tale*:
▷ Robert Silverberg, *A Time Of Changes*

STABLEFORD, Brian M(ichael) (born 1948)
British novelist, short story writer and critic

Stableford writes imaginative, ingenious stories about the biology, sociology and ecology of alien worlds, reminiscent of ▷ Niven's approach to physics. His two major series are the Hooded Swan (beginning with *Halcyon Drift*, 1972), describing the adventures of the cynical star-pilot Grainger and his alien symbiote, and the Daedalus Mission (beginning with *The Florians*, 1976), about a spaceship sent to recontact colonies which have lost touch with Earth.

READ·ON

● *Man In A Cage*
▶ ▷ Orson Scott Card, *Speaker For The Dead*
▷ Brian Aldiss, *Helliconia Spring*
▷ Frank Herbert, *The Green Brain*
▷ George R R Martin, *Tuf Voyaging*

STAPLEDON, Olaf (1886–1950)
British novelist

Stapledon explored his major interest, the philosophy of religion, in many works, from the non-fiction *Beyond The 'Isms'* (1942) to novels such as *Star Maker* (1937), which powerfully describes the rise of a cosmic civilisation through the evolution of millions of different species, each of which makes up only a tiny fraction of the total Mind which struggles against the imperfection and entropic doom of the universe to discover and understand its Creator. *Odd John* (1935), the story of present day supermen who despite their intelligence and spiritual achievement are destroyed by our own race, prefigures many of *Star Maker*'s themes, including its emphasis on the ecstasy of mental communion and the inability of ordinary minds to comprehend the ultimate. *Sirius* (1944), Stapledon's most sensitively told novel, is the story of a dog enhanced to human intelligence and his relationship with the woman brought up as his sister. *Last And First Men* (1930) is the history of the eighteen stages of humanity, from our own (the first) to a highly evolved species which becomes extinct in two billion years' time on the planet Neptune. Despite occasional clumsiness of expression, it is full of original and influential ideas, and has a rare sense of grandeur.

READ·ON
- *Last Men In London* (the views of a Last Man on Earth in Stapledon's time)
  The Flames
- ▷ Doris Lessing, *Shikasta*
- To *Odd John*:
  - ▷ H G Wells, *The Food Of The Gods*
  - ▷ Theodore Sturgeon, *More Than Human*

STERLING, Bruce (born 1954)
US novelist and short story writer

Sterling believes that sf should form a pop literature of ideas, 'a mass reaction to social change', and his writing puts this belief into practice. Fascinated by technology and its possibilities, Sterling writes of original and interesting ideas in a fast-moving style which brings his vision of the future to vivid life. His first book, *Involution Ocean* (1977, about the sailors on the dust oceans of inhospitable Nullaqua) was followed by *The Artificial Kid* (1980), the fast-plotted story of a star of media violence who cannot bear to be deprived of his audience. Sterling's best-known book is *Schismatrix* (1985), which tells the story of 140 years of a man's life, against the background of a Solar System divided between the Mechanists (who integrate themselves with cybernetic machinery and computers) and the Shapers (who use drugs and genetic engineering to enhance their capabilities). The book follows the changes undergone by the human race as they begin to force their evolution into totally different physical forms, and eventually into another order of being.

READ·ON
- *Islands In The Net* (set in a future where the world's communication systems have been integrated into one vast 'Net')

▶   Other modern pop literature ('cyberpunk'):
▷ William Gibson, *Neuromancer*
Michael Swanwick, *Vacuum Flowers*
▶ ▷ Alfred Bester, *The Demolished Man*
▷ John Varley, *In The Hall Of The Martian Kings*

STRUGATSKY, Arkady (born 1925) **and Boris** (born 1931)
Russian novelists

The Strugatskys' early novels (written, as always, in collaboration) are entertaining stories of space exploration, set in a utopian future. Later works are thematically more complex, typical of much Eastern European sf in their underlying humanist ethics and lack of interest in detailed backgrounds. Examples include *Hard To Be A God* (1964), describing the mental agonies of Earth agents trying to civilise a savage, medieval world without destroying its culture by obvious interference, and the related *Prisoners Of Power* (1971), the alternately amusing and disturbing story of a superhumanly able innocent's slow education in the realities of power and government. *Roadside Picnic* (1972) is perhaps the most profound of these novels, dealing with the results of an extraterrestrial visitation which leaves the Earth's surface littered with bizarre 'zones' containing both great dangers and vast treasures – including a device to grant any wish. *The Snail On The Slope* (1966–8) is a ▷ Kafkaesque tale of scientific investigation and existential bewilderment, full of strange and powerful images. The novel is the interwoven stories of Kandid, who struggles to gain some understanding of the totally alien Forest in which he is trapped, and Pepper, locked in desperate and eventually futile combat with the bizarre scientific bureaucracy which is supposedly trying to understand the Forest.

READ·ON   ●   'The Second Martian Invasion' (in Bearne ed, *Vortex*) demonstrates the Strugatskys' gift for rural settings.
Far Rainbow
▶ ▷ Stanislaw Lem, *Solaris*
▶   To *Roadside Picnic*:
▷ Frederik Pohl, *Gateway*

STURGEON, Theodore (1918–85)
US novelist and short story writer

Sturgeon's short stories range from the unsettling horror of 'Bianca's Hands' (which have a life independent of Bianca's will, gaining her a husband with their beauty and then killing him to consummate the marriage) in *E Pluribus Unicorn* (1959) through the romantic fantasy and off-beat humour of 'To Here

And The Easel' (paralleling fantasy and everyday life in its description of two kinds of love) in *To Here And The Easel* (1973) to the psychologically based sf of 'The World Well Lost' (a sympathetic story of homosexuality, very unusual for its time) in *Starshine* (1966). All his work shows a gentle and humane sensitivity; a sense of the terror of loneliness and of the need for love which has rarely been surpassed. *More Than Human* (1953) is the story of a group of psionically gifted social outcasts who join together mentally to become a new kind of symbiotic organism, within which they are no longer alone. The book deals powerfully with the creature's struggles to be born, and its eventual attainment of maturity.

R E A D • O N

- ● *Venus Plus X* (a powerful if sentimental examination of gender roles)
- ▶ To the short stories:
  - ▷ Samuel Delany, *Driftglass*
  - ▷ James Tiptree, *Warm Worlds And Otherwise*
  - Kit Reed, *The Killer Mice*
- ▶ To *More Than Human*:
  - ▷ Keith Roberts, *The Inner Wheel*

SWORD AND SORCERY
- Steven Brust, *Jhereg*
- ▷ Lin Carter, *The Warrior Of World's End*
- ▷ Robert E Howard, *Conan Of Cimmeria*
- John Jakes, *Brak The Barbarian*
- ▷ Fritz Leiber, *Swords Against Death*
- ▷ Michael Moorcock, *The Bull And The Spear*
- C L Moore, *Jirel Of Joiry*
- Karl Edward Wagner, *Bloodstone*
- ▷ Roger Zelazny, *Dilvish The Damned*

T

THEATRES OF THE ABSURD
- ▷ J G Ballard, *Concrete Island*
- ▷ John Barth, *Lost In The Funhouse*
- Donald Barthelme, *Great Days*
- Italo Calvino, *Cosmicomics*
- George Alec Effinger, *What Entropy Means To Me*

▷ Franz Kafka, *The Trial*
▷ Thomas Pynchon, *Gravity's Rainbow*
▷ Robert Sheckley, *Options*
▷ John Sladek, *Keep The Giraffe Burning*

TIME
▷ Isaac Asimov, *The End Of Eternity*
▷ Barrington J Bayley, *Collision With Chronos*
▷ Philip K Dick, *Ubik*
▷ Alan Garner, *Red Shift*
  David Gerrold, *The Man Who Folded Himself*
▷ Joe Haldeman, *The Forever War*
▷ Michael Moorcock, *An Alien Heat*
  Ward Moore, *Bring The Jubilee*
▷ Tim Powers, *The Anubis Gates*
  Wilson Tucker, *The Year Of The Quiet Sun*

TIPTREE Jr, James (1915–1987)
US short story writer and novelist

Alice Sheldon (who wrote as James Tiptree Jr, and occasionally as Raccoona Sheldon) wrote stories dealing with a wide range of human experience, distinguished by their understanding of all people and all points of view. She frequently displays a preoccupation with the symbolic value of the alien, presented as a terrifying threat in such stories as 'The Screwfly Solution' (where aliens release a virus that makes the male sexual response automatically murderous, in *Out Of The Everywhere*, 1981) and as saviour in 'Beam Us Home' (the moving story of a young American whose violent surroundings force him to identify with imaginary aliens, in *Ten Thousand Light Years From Home*, 1973). Among Tiptree's best stories are 'Houston, Houston, Do You Read?', describing the reactions of three of today's astronauts transplanted to a future where only women exist (in *Star Songs of an Old Primate*, 1978), and 'The Girl who was Plugged In', dealing metaphorically with the modern cult of media image, while also demonstrating Tiptree's strong feeling for technique (in *Warm Worlds and Otherwise*, 1975).

READ·ON

● *Up The Walls Of The World*, *Brightness Falls From The Air* and *The Starry Rift* (collection) are space opera pastiches, gentler if less profound than her earlier short stories; *Tales Of The Quintana Roo* (collection).

▶ Short stories reflecting Tiptree's humane concerns:

▷ Theodore Sturgeon, *A Touch of Sturgeon*
Connie Willis, *Firewatch*
Karen Joy Fowler, *Artificial Things*
Pamela Sargent, *Starshadows*
▶ To her feminism:
Joanna Russ, *Extra(Ordinary) People*

TOLKIEN, J(ohn) R(onald) R(euel) (1892–1973)
South African/British novelist

Although Tolkien did not invent the heroic fantasy genre – far from it – his writing is almost single-handedly responsible for its tremendous current popularity. His fantasy world, Middle-Earth, was far more detailed and sustained than those of earlier authors. It was originally conceived as a backdrop for linguistic experimentation. He was a professor of Anglo-Saxon at the University of Oxford, profoundly interested in philology. Development and evolution of languages led to a history of racial movements, then to a mythology and detailed history, then to two novels – *The Hobbit* (1937) and *The Lord of the Rings* (1954–5). This gradual creation process is fascinatingly reconstructed in *Unfinished Tales* (1980) and *The Book of Lost Tales* (1983–4), collections of posthumous gleanings from Tolkien's notes by his son Christopher. Much of the mythology and historical legend behind the novels is presented in *The Silmarillion* (1977), an Old Testament of Middle-Earth. Connected poems are in *The Adventures of Tom Bombadil* (1962), and songs in *The Road Goes Ever On* (1968) (with Donald Swann). Tolkien was an associate at Oxford of ▷ C S Lewis and Charles Williams, and although Christianity is less obtrusive in his work than theirs, his morality is similarly simple and straightforward: his heroes are heroes, his villains, villains. There is no satirical intent; the books can be read purely as an escape to a refreshingly straightforward world, one which has much in common with the naïve, romantic image of medieval 'Merrie England'.

THE HOBBIT, OR THERE AND BACK AGAIN (1937)
Bilbo Baggins, the 'hobbit' of the title, is disturbed from his quiet, comfortable life by the wizard Gandalf, who conscripts him into a party of dwarves bent on regaining their ancestral treasures from the dragon Smaug. Their journey is beset by such hazards as trolls, giant spiders, wolves, goblins and the like; Bilbo finds hidden depths within himself, realising that he must betray his friends the dwarves to avoid conflict over the treasure once the dragon is killed. Originally written for children, *The Hobbit* avoids the moralising of the later *The Lord of the Rings,* and is more tightly plotted. The slightly simplistic characters have an impact born of familiarity, as they draw heavily upon figures of myth. In both this and the later book, Tolkien handles his heroic themes with an ease matched by few of his imitators.

Tolkien's other work includes the children's books Farmer Giles of Ham, Smith of Wootton Major *and* The Father Christmas Letters.

READ•ON ● *The Lord Of The Rings is an heroic account of war between good and evil, mixed with more human passages as we see the hobbit Frodo penetrate to the heart of Sauron's empire to destroy the One Ring.*

▶ ▷ Guy Gavriel Kay, *The Summer Tree*
Cherry Wilder, *A Princess Of The Chameln*
Judith Tarr, *The Isle Of Glass*

▶ Harvard Lampoon, *Bored Of The Rings* (an hilarious parody)

▷ David Eddings, *Pawn Of Prophecy* (a faithful homage to the Master)

TRAVELOGUES
▷ Hal Clement, *Mission Of Gravity*
▷ Philip José Farmer, *Maker Of Universes*
▷ Larry Niven, *Ringworld*
▷ Robert Silverberg, *Lord Valentine's Castle*
▷ Jack Vance, *City Of The Chasch*
▷ Gene Wolfe, *The Book Of The New Sun*

TUBB, E(dwin) C(harles) (born 1919)
British novelist

Tubb's most widely-read work, the Dumarest series (starting with *Goth*, 1968), follows the itinerant hero Earl Dumarest in his search for his home planet, Earth. In each book Dumarest arrives at a new planet, has various adventures while failing to find any useful information as to Earth's location, and leaves again. Heroic fantasy at its most traditional, the series appeals to those who prefer their adventures uncluttered by literary merit and sexual equality. Tubb's other works include, under the pseudonym Gregory Kern, another wide-ranging series featuring secret agent Cap Kennedy (beginning with *Galaxy Of The Lost*, 1973).

READ•ON ▶ Robert Adams, *The Coming Of The Horseclans*
▷ Robert Howard, *Conan The Conqueror*

TURNER, George (born 1916)
Australian novelist and short story writer

Turner writes novels of character set in the not too distant future. The

Beloved Son trilogy (*Beloved Son, Vaneglory* and *Yesterday's Men,* 1978–83) deals with the gradual rebuilding of society over the next century, following a nuclear holocaust. *The Sea And Summer* (1987) is a richly characterised story of the widening gulf between the 'haves' and 'have nots' in near-future Melbourne as rising seas caused by the greenhouse effect make life in the poor areas ever more difficult.

READ•ON
► To *Beloved Son*:
▷ Walter M Miller, *A Canticle For Leibowitz*
Robie MacAuley, *A Secret History Of Time To Come*
► To *The Sea And Summer*:
▷ Angela Carter, *Heroes And Villains*
▷ John Brunner, *The Sheep Look Up*

V

VANCE, Jack (born 1920)
US novelist and short story writer

Vance's writing is distinguished by literary quality, irony and exotic, unpredictable phraseology. His protagonists are not taciturn Conans but instead charming and erudite men, often endowed with biting wit; these qualities frequently extend to his chief villains, relieving the reader from the tedium of always hearing the same boring and bloodthirsty threats. The subject matter of Vance's works varies from the hard sf of the Durdane novels (such as *The Anome*) to the baroque and inventive fantasies of *The Dying Earth* (1950) and its sequels, but in all these it is the human qualities of the characters which attract the reader's sympathy. The epic Lyonesse series begins with *Lyonesse I: Suldrun's Garden* (1983), an intricately plotted fantasy set in the Enchanted Isles, imaginary lands southwest of Dark Age Britain. The power struggle between the once united countries of the Isles forms the basis of the novel, which follows the fortunes of Prince Aillas of Troicenet as he seeks his lost son Dhrun. Vance has skilfully interwoven elements of Celtic, Norse and Greek myths with his own fantastic invention to produce a moving and compelling story.

READ•ON
● *The Eyes Of The Overworld*
The Languages Of Pao (concerned with how the language people speak can compel them to think in certain ways)
The Star King

▶ To Vance's fantasy:
  Michael Shea, *Nifft The Lean*
▷ Tanith Lee, *Cyrion*
▷ Fritz Leiber, *Swords Against Death*
▶ To his sf:
▷ M John Harrison, *The Pastel City*

VAN VOGT, A(lfred) E(lton) (born 1912)
Canadian/US novelist and short story writer

Van Vogt's stories are colourful adventures, animated by a feverish flow of ideas. Most of his books are compelling wish fulfilment, featuring isolated and oppressed supermen with whom the reader is meant to identify. The best example is probably *Slan* (1946), which describes the adolescence of a superintelligent mutant with telepathic powers. Similarly, *The Weapon Shops of Isher* (1951) and its sequel *The Weapon Makers* (1946) feature an immortal protagonist who has created both the authoritarian imperial government and its enemy, the Weapon Shops (which act to preserve individual freedom). The Null-A books (*The World of Null-A,* 1948, *The Players of Null-A,* 1956, and *Null-A Three,* 1985) feature a pseudo-science called General Semantics, which proposes a non-Aristotelian attitude to reality (one unrestricted by yes/no logic). In the first book the hero Gilbert Gosseyn ('go sane'), General Semanticist extraordinaire, first finds that his memory is a fabrication, then that he has an extra brain with unknown powers, and finally that whenever he dies a clone with his memories takes his place – and van Vogt has only just begun . . .

READ·ON ● *The Voyage Of The Space Beagle* (space opera involving interesting shipboard politics)
  Empire of The Atom
  The War Against The Rull
▶ To the resurrection in the Null-A books:
▷ John Varley, *The Ophiuchi Hotline*
▶ To the power fantasy:
▷ E E Smith, *Children Of The Lens*
▷ Roger Zelazny, *Nine Princes In Amber*

VARLEY, John (born 1947)
US novelist and short story writer

Most of Varley's work is set in an original and detailed common future in which aliens have defeated mankind and ceded Earth to whales and dolphins, leaving human refugees scattered throughout the Solar System. Varley uses this setting to explore the effects of technological development on both society and individuals, through such stories as the excellent 'Equinoctial' (describing the experience of life as a genetically engineered human-plant symbiote among the rings of Saturn, in *Picnic On Nearside/The Barbie Murders*). Varley focuses especially on the changes in sexual mores resulting from easily available gender changes (also examined in 'Options', from *Blue Champagne*, 1986). *The Ophiuchi Hotline* (1977) is a novel with the same background, involving almost all the ideas from the short stories (for example, all facets of the plot are told from the points of view of different clones of the same person) and providing a final explanation for Earth's conquest. Like much of Varley's work, this novel is a superb example of recent sf which uses new ideas to generate the same sense of wonder as stories from the Golden Age did when still fresh.

READ·ON   ● The Gaean trilogy (*Titan, Wizard* and *Demon*; fantasy within a sf framework set in a vast spaceship-world, describing the long struggle between an immortal human and the god-like but increasingly mad world mind) *In The Hall Of The Martian Kings* (collection)
▶ ▷ Joe Haldeman, *Mindbridge*
  ▷ Larry Niven, *A Gift From Earth*
  ▷ Gregory Benford, *Against Infinity*

VERNE, Jules (1828–1905)
French novelist and playwright

One of the pioneers of the sf of ideas, Verne uses technological advances to reveal hitherto inaccessible vistas of wonder. In *Around The World In Eighty Days* Phileas Fogg makes the journey of the title by balloon, while the Baltimore Gun Club's spaceship is fired by a cannon From *The Earth To The Moon* (1865). Verne's earliest writing shows an almost childlike faith in the beneficence of scientific progress, with humanity conquering the elements in its individualistic quest for knowledge. It is only in later works such as *Twenty Thousand Leagues Under The Sea* (1870) and *The Clipper Of The Clouds* (1886) that he expresses reservations about the uncontrolled advance of technology. In *Twenty Thousand Leagues,* a vessel investigating attacks on shipping by a giant sea monster is itself sunk and the survivors are taken on board the submarine *Nautilus,* which is responsible for the incidents. Its commander, the melancholy and embittered Captain Nemo, who has rejected the world above, gives a guided tour of the ocean's marvels. *Twenty Thousand Leagues* ushers in Verne's darker, mature period; Nemo's character, actions and motivations are far more equivocal than those of his predecessors.

READ·ON   ● In *Master of the World*, Verne's bleakest work, the mad inventor Robur takes Nemo's

misanthropy a stage further.
Five Weeks In A Balloon
Journey To The Centre Of The Earth
▶ To the early novels:
▷ Arthur C Clarke, Rendezvous With Rama
Sir Arthur Conan Doyle, *The Lost World*
▶ To the late novels:
▷ H G Wells, *The Island Of Dr Moreau*

VONNEGUT, Kurt (born 1922)
US novelist and short story writer

To Vonnegut, all humanity is a ridiculous joke – but ultimately the joke is sour, the humour bitter and often despairing. He has no faith in science, religion, governments or charities, only in the efforts of individual men and women – and, in the end, even they are often overwhelmed by the world they struggle against. Bizarre imagination marks his sf; a talent for peculiarly amusing ideas that carry within them the seeds of a profound re-evaluation of our lives. So *Cat's Cradle* (1963) features a religion of deliberate hypocrisy, whose leader Bokonon advocates the use of foma ('harmless untruths') and communal sacrament by mutual foot rubbing. Vonnegut's non-sf works approach the themes of his sf from different angles, as in *God Bless You, Mr Rosewater* (1965), where one man, ridiculed and misunderstood by his peers, sets about becoming a genuine humanitarian. In Vonnegut's own words, 'My books are essentially mosaics made up of a whole bunch of tiny chips, and each chip is a joke.'

THE SIRENS OF TITAN (1959)
Malachi Constant, the luckiest person in the world, is invited to attend one of the periodic appearances on Earth of the rich adventurer Niles Rumfoord. Rumfoord is trapped in a 'chrono-synclastic infundibulum' which dooms him to manifest on any solid body intersecting the spiral path he traces through the Solar System – a condition which means that he must live every instant of his life simultaneously, shattering all his illusions of free will and enabling him to predict Malachi's eventual marriage to Rumfoord's wife. Horrified by Rumfoord's prophecies, Malachi attempts to flee his fate – but in the process condemns himself to act it out, on a bizarre tour of the Solar System that takes him from the radio-controlled soldiers of Mars to the living 'harmoniums' of Mercury. During his wanderings Malachi fulfils Rumfoord's plan for the salvation of Earth, leading eventually to its domination by the Church Of God The Utterly Indifferent (which makes 'all men truly equal' by handicapping any with exceptional abilities) – but is the plan truly Rumfoord's, or is he, too, trapped by the impersonal forces of predestination?

Vonnegut's other works include Breakfast Of Champions, Bluebeard, Player

Piano, Mother Night *(in which an American ex-Nazi, and secret agent for the US, struggles to find his true identity), and* Welcome To The Monkey House *(a collection including 'Harrison Bergeron', an amusing reappraisal of the likely fate of a genuine superman).*

READ·ON

● *Slaughterhouse-5* (which further explores the concern with free will shown in *The Sirens Of Titan*)

Galápagos (in which humanity is saved from the consequences of its own folly by evolving into a seal-like species which lacks the big brains that have hampered humans throughout history)

▶ ▷ Philip José Farmer, *Venus On The Half-Shell*
▶ James Morrow, *This Is The Way The World Ends*
▷ John Sladek, *Roderick*
▷ Robert Sheckley, *Journey Beyond Tomorrow*
▷ Thomas Pynchon, *The Crying Of Lot 49*
John Irving, *The Hotel New Hampshire*
Joseph Heller, *Catch-22*
▶ To the predestination in *The Sirens Of Titan*:
▷ Robert Silverberg, *The Stochastic Man*

W

WAR

▷ Orson Scott Card, *Ender's Game*
Glen Cook, *The Black Company*
▷ Joe Haldeman, *The Forever War*
▷ Harry Harrison, *Bill, The Galactic Hero*
▷ Robert Heinlein, *Starship Troopers*
▷ Michael Moorcock, *My Experiences In The Third World War*
Alan Moore with Ian Gibson, *The Ballad Of Halo Jones Book 3* (graphic novel)
▷ Fred Saberhagen, *The Berserker Wars*
▷ Lucius Shepard, *Life During Wartime*

WATSON, Ian (born 1943)
British novelist and short story writer

Despite sometimes stiff style and rather weak characterisation, Watson's books are highly inventive, containing vivid, occasionally disturbing imagery. His early novels discuss the nature of perception, often in metaphysical terms; in *The Jonah Kit* (1975), our universe is discovered (by whales) to be no more than a shadow of the 'real' one, while *Miracle Visitors* (1978) explores the inherent inexplicability of certain phenomena. Watson has also written many excellent short stories, among them 'The Very Slow Time Machine' (about a time machine catapulted into the future via the past, in the eponymous collection, 1979). *The Book of the River* (1984) tells the story of Yaleen, born on the banks of a river along the centre of which runs the black current which forms one boundary of her world, and on which only women can sail without going mad. Yaleen herself becomes a riverwoman before the black current withdraws from the river, leading to her people's invasion by the male-dominated Sons of Adam from the other bank. Sequels are *The Book Of The Stars* (1984) and *The Book Of Being* (1985).

READ • ON
- ● *God's World* (aliens call humanity to an appointment with God)
  The Martian Inca and *The Embedding* also deal with perception, while more recent work uses the framework of horror, often (as in *The Fire Worm*) to explore themes of sexuality
- ▶ To the horror:
  - ▷ Iain Banks, *The Wasp Factory*
- ▶ To the early novels:
  - ▷ Frank Herbert, *Destination: Voi*
  - ▷ Thomas M Disch, *Camp Concentration*

WEIRD SCIENCE/WORLDS
- ▷ Greg Bear, *Eon*
- ▷ James Blish, *Cities In Flight*
- ▷ Hal Clement, *Close To Critical*
- ▷ Robert L Forward, *Dragon's Egg*
  David Langford, *The Space Eater*
- ▷ Christopher Priest, *Inverted World*
- ▷ Rudy Rucker, *White Light*
- ▷ Bob Shaw, *The Ragged Astronauts*

WELLS, H(erbert) G(eorge) (1866–1946)
British writer of novels, short stories and non-fiction

One of the most influential figures in the development of sf, Wells introduced many now common sf themes: time travel (in *The Time Machine*, 1895), alien invasion (in *The War Of The Worlds*, 1898), biological reconstruction (in *The Island Of Dr Moreau*, 1896), giant insects (in *The Food of the Gods*, 1904), atomic holocaust (in *The World Set Free*, 1914). Wells was in his youth a student of the Darwinian scientist T H Huxley, and much of his writing (including *The Time Machine, A Modern Utopia, Men Like Gods, The Shape Of Things To Come*) deals with the evolution of the human species and of society along Darwinian lines. The first story to visualise time as a fourth dimension, and thus to conceive of mechanical movement along it, *The Time Machine* concerns an inventor who travels forward in time and observes the future of human society. He finds humanity divided; the androgynous Eloi live in a pastoral wonderland, subsisting on fruit, while the bestial Morlocks inhabit industrialised underground caves. Here Wells makes points about Victorian class relationships, although more of the book's interest lies in the Time Traveller's discovery of how future humanity has forsaken its heritage. *The Time Machine* is typical of Wells' constant dilemma; socialism led him to hope for a better future, while Darwinism grimly stifled this hope.

READ·ON ▶ To Wells' evolutionary ideas:
▷ Olaf Stapledon, *Last And First Men*
▷ C S Lewis, *That Hideous Strength*
▷ Robert Heinlein, *The Moon Is A Harsh Mistress*
▶ To *The Time Machine*:
Wilson Tucker, *The Year Of The Quiet Sun*
▷ Christopher Priest, *The Space Machine* (an impressive pastiche)

WHITE, T(erence) H(anbury) (1906–64)
British novelist

White's pacifist beliefs find ample expression in his Arthurian fantasy *The Once And Future King* (1958), stories which bring the period to vivid life by the use of anachronistic parallels to increase our empathy with the characters. The first volume describes Arthur's life up to his accession; its central theme is improving humanity via the study of other creatures. This is revisited in the fifth book, while intervening volumes treat the classic Arthurian legends with characteristic knockabout humour. Compassion for their victims inspires the King's ultimately futile desire for peace through true chivalry. The normal edition (1958) contains four individual books, with *The Book Of Merlyn* (1978), the fifth, published separately.

READ·ON   ▶   Thomas Malory, *Le Morte D'Arthur* (a rather less accessible account of the 'Matter of Britain')
▷ Marion Zimmer Bradley, *The Mists Of Avalon*
Nikolai Tolstoy, *The Coming Of The King*
John Steinbeck, *The Acts Of King Arthur And His Noble Knights*

WILHELM, Kate (born 1928)
US novelist and short story writer

Wilhelm's work explores the feelings of realistic people with sensitivity and insight, placing them in a wide range of convincing situations. In *Juniper Time* (1979) a message which may be from aliens is discovered in a USA undergoing a lengthy drought, while *Where Late The Sweet Birds Sang* (1976) is set in a post-holocaust America inhabited by humans brought up as groups of identical clones, whose psychological differences from ordinary humanity are the focal point of the story. Her most recent novel, *Huysman's Pets* (1986), is about secret research into ESP between genetically engineered twins.

READ·ON   ●   *Fault Lines*
The Clewiston Test
The Infinity Box (collection)
▶ ▷ Ursula K LeGuin, *The Dispossessed*

WILSON, Robert Anton (born 1932)
US novelist

Wilson's optimistic visions of a 'hedonic revolution' are expressed in a number of linked books, revolving around the *Illuminatus!* trilogy (1975; see below). The most explicit descriptions of his programme come in the essay collection *The Illuminati Papers* (1980) and the trilogy *Schrödinger's Cat* (comprising *The Universe Next Door*, *The Trick Top Hat* and *The Homing Pigeons*, 1981). The latter uses quantum mechanics as a metaphor for the possibilities of the human future, with Wilson firmly in favour of an anarchist society with space exploration and plenty of mind-expanding chemicals. The trilogy is a refreshingly naïve, encouragingly positive conception of what the future has to offer. The *Illuminatus!* trilogy (*The Eye In The Pyramid*, *The Golden Apple* and *Leviathan*), credited to Robert Shea and Wilson, is a dazzling psychedelic fantasy which has the world in the grip of such rival secret societies as the Discordians, the Justified Ancients of Mummu, and of course the ancient Illuminati themselves. Fragmented, stream-of-consciousness writing disorients the reader, helping Wilson mix fact and fiction indistinguishably. This is the principle of 'guerilla ontology', assaulting readers' ideas of what is or is not true, forcing them to think it out, and making the trilogy as stimulating as it is funny.

READ·ON
- ● *Masks Of The Illuminati*
- ▶ ▷ William Burroughs, *Cities Of The Red Night*
- ▷ Thomas Pynchon, *The Crying Of Lot 49*
- Malaclypse the Younger, *Principia Discordia*

WOLFE, Gene (born 1931)
US novelist and short story writer

Ever since *The Fifth Head Of Cerberus* (1972), a subtle and thoughtful collection of three linked novellas, Wolfe has enjoyed immense critical acclaim. His talents are as diverse as they are prodigious. *Soldier Of The Mist* (1986), which to some extent mirrors *The Book Of The New Sun* (see below), is a fantasy set in the ancient Greece of Herodotus about a man incapable of retaining any memory for over eight hours. *Free Live Free* (1984) is a Wizard of Oz fairy tale crossed with Dashiell Hammett and a touch of time travel. *The Devil In A Forest* (1976) is an ambiguous and richly characterised juvenile medieval fantasy. The outstanding, poetic *Peace* (1975) drifts through the memories of the ghost of an ordinary man, imbuing them with the beauty and complexity so typical of the author. *Operation ARES* (1970) is a conventional sf adventure novel. Wolfe's short stories exhibit even greater variety; for instance, the Island/Doctor/Death trilogy presents ambiguous and complementary images of isolation and the healer, while 'Forlesen' (in *Gene Wolfe's Book Of Days*, 1981) is a surreal tale of ▷ Dickian alienation. Nevertheless, many themes are common in his work, primarily that of identity, especially in so far as it relates to time and memory. Wolfe's writing, characterised by a remarkable literacy and depth, never becomes pompous or unapproachable, thanks in part to the gentle wit which pervades it.

THE BOOK OF THE NEW SUN (1980–3)
Prophetically if prematurely hailed as the major sf work of the 1980s, this tetralogy (*The Shadow Of The Torturer, The Claw Of The Conciliator, The Sword Of The Lictor* and *The Citadel Of The Autarch*) sealed Wolfe's critical and popular success. Its youthful hero, Severian, is expelled from the Guild of Torturers and forced to explore the far-future 'Urth' which he inhabits. The action takes place against the vividly described and endlessly intriguing backdrop of Urth under its dying sun, but it is often held up while Severian recounts children's tales or the texts of plays, or for his metaphysical speculations. Severian's journey is also closely tied up with the religion, a far-distant relative of Christianity based around the expectation of a messiah (the Conciliator reborn) who will bring, and is in some way identified with, the New Sun. As the tetralogy proceeds, Severian progresses from torturer to lictor (executioner) to Autarch – and ultimately, it is implied, to Conciliator.

Gene WOLFE • *The Book Of The New Sun*

Landscapes Of Decay

▷ Jorge Luis BORGES
LABYRINTHS
*(an anthology of Borges' 'fictions', many
dealing with the metaphysics of Life
and Art)*

▷ Stanislaw LEM
A PERFECT VACUUM
*(reviews of non-existent books, including
many interesting ideas about meaning and
information)*

Books About Books About. . .

Laurence STERNE
TRISTRAM SHANDY
*(a spectacular shaggy-dog novel – of life
inside a novel)*

▷ John BARTH
CHIMERA
*(Life tries to imitate Art – with
embarrassingly scant success)*

▷ Christopher PRIEST
THE AFFIRMATION
*(a writer redefines himself, his friends and
family, and ultimately his entire world)*

Marcel PROUST
**REMEMBRANCE OF THINGS
PAST**
*(vast and detailed meditation on how
mundane life acquires meaning through
memory)*

▷ Philip K DICK
A SCANNER DARKLY
*(the dual life of a narc – which of his
identities is the 'real' one?)*

Memory And Identity

▷ Robert SHECKLEY
MINDSWAP
*(Marvin Flynn is forced to take body after
increasingly strange body in the quest to
recover his own)*

▷ Christopher PRIEST
THE GLAMOUR
*(amnesiac haunted by his possible pasts –
and not wishing to confront the real one)*

▷ John BARTH
GILES GOAT-BOY
*(rejection and ridicule of a Christ figure in
a close parody of 1960s America)*

▷ M John HARRISON
IN VIRICONIUM
*(will the drunken gods of the city stop
inventing Chinese takeaways long enough
to save it from a disease of decay?)*

▷ Stephen DONALDSON
**THE CHRONICLES OF THOMAS
COVENANT**
*(leper is brought from Earth to be the
reluctant redeemer of a fantasy world)*

Messiah And Redeemer

▷ Richard COWPER
THE ROAD TO CORLAY
*(the death of a boy piper sparks off a
peace-loving rival to the Church Militant)*

▷ Richard ADAMS
SHARDIK
*(a giant bear becomes a symbol for a
barbaric conquest, but later achieves true
redeemer status and inspires a peaceful
religion)*

▷ Michael MOORCOCK
THE STEALER OF SOULS
*(Elric is exiled from his homeland first
by his cousin, then by his revenge – the
destruction of the entire nation)*

▷ Roger ZELAZNY
NINE PRINCES IN AMBER
*(Prince Corwin is thrown from Amber into
a shadow-world – our own – by his
scheming brothers)*

Exiles

▷ Robert SILVERBERG
HAWKSBILL STATION
*(political prisoners exiled to Earth's distant
past)*

Walter TEVIS
THE MAN WHO FELL TO EARTH
*(alien from high-technology dying world
comes to Earth for help – with tragic
results)*

Dense and complex though it is, this is no sterile intellectual game: so many ideas – above and beyond the running theme of identity, and the messianic myth – crowd into Wolfe's text that the tetralogy is like a library in itself. There are more wonders, mysteries and subtleties in a single chapter than in most writers' complete novels.

More of Wolfe's stories are collected in The Island Of Doctor Death And Other Stories And Other Stories. The Urth Of The New Sun *continues Severian's story along new thematic lines.*

READ·ON   ▶   To *Peace*:
Marcel Proust, *Time Regained* (part 7 of *Remembrance Of Things Past*)
▷ John Crowley, *Aegypt*
▷ Alan Garner, *The Stone Book Quartet*
▷ John Barth, *Chimera*
▶ To *Soldier Of The Mist*:
Oliver Sacks, *The Man Who Mistook His Wife For A Hat*
Other classical fantasies include
▷ Naomi Mitchison, *The Corn King And The Spring Queen*
Thomas Burnett Swann, *Day Of The Minotaur*
Robert Graves, *The Golden Fleece*
Mary Renault, *The Bull From The Sea*
For source material, see Herodotus, *Histories*

WYNDHAM, John (1903–1969)
British novelist and short story writer

Wyndham's stories are usually based upon a single idea or change in the world, frequently involving the breakdown of society, but always with an up-beat resolution. In *The Day Of The Triffids* (1951), disaster is caused by a comet that blinds all but a few people; the survivors are then targets for triffids (large mobile plants) which are described in a truly terrifying manner. *The Midwich Cuckoos* (1959) describes the consequences of the entire female population of an English village bearing non-human offspring. Wyndham's short story collections, notably *The Seeds Of Time* (1957) and *Consider Her Ways And Others* (1961), contain many ingenious ideas; 'Consider Her Ways' itself is one of the first stories to compare an all female future society not unfavourably with ours. The future of *The Chrysalids* (1955) is one of frequent genetic mutations hunted down ruthlessly by a puritanical church. David, born into a particularly strict family, finds that he and some of his peers can communicate telepathically. Eventually they are discovered and have to flee for their lives, pursued by their own parents. The novel beautifully describes the childrens' telepathic relationship, and makes a strong case for change over stability.

READ•ON
- ● *Chocky* (the story of a little boy's friend who isn't as imaginary as everyone thinks)
  The Kraken Wakes
- ▶ To *The Day Of The Triffids*:
  - ▷ Algis Budrys, *Some Will Not Die*
  - ▷ J G Ballard, *The Wind From Nowhere*
- ▶ To *The Chrysalids*:
  - ▷ Theodore Sturgeon, *More Than Human*
- ◊ Catastrophes

WYNNE JONES, Diana
British novelist

Wynne Jones writes originally for young people, but her complexity of theme and treatment, and her depth of characterisation speak to all readers. Her inventive and intelligent use of sf and fantasy material adds spice to her work. *Eight Days Of Luke* (1975), for example, is an unusual updating of Norse myth, while *Dogsbody* (1975) has the spirit of the star Sirius confined within the form of a dog. She delights in exploring murky personal relationships and in dashing perceptions; protagonists are often struggling for acceptance in an oppressive world, and triumph over adversity by discovering hidden reserves of ability. *Charmed Life* (1977) and its sequels amusingly study a society like our own, but with magic, while *Power Of Three* (1976) and *Cart And Cwidder* (1975) deal with the awakening of local powers.

READ•ON
- ● *The Spellcoats*
  The Ogre Downstairs
- ▶ Joan Aiken, *Night Birds On Nantucket*
  - ▷ Alan Garner, *The Owl Service*

Z

ZAMYATIN, Yevgeny (1884–1937)
Russian novelist and short story writer

Originally a committed Communist, Zamyatin became increasingly disenchanted with aspects of the October Revolution, an attitude that inspired him to write his sf novel *We* (1924). This book presents an extreme image of the absolute world state, told by one of its citizens in a language whose use of solely scientific and mathematical metaphor demonstrates his emotional and artistic poverty. The novel's main purpose is to dramatise this loss, the result of the near total victory of rational thought with no other purpose than maintaining and propagating itself.

READ·ON   ▶ ▷ Aldous Huxley, *Brave New World*
                ▷ George Orwell, *1984*
                Ivan Yefremov, *Andromeda* is an alternative vision, a Marxist utopia.

ZELAZNY, Roger (born 1937)
US novelist and short story writer

The hallmark of Zelazny's work is his blend of scientific backgrounds with themes from myth. In *Lord Of Light* (1967), for example, the central characters use psionics and technology to become avatars of the Hindu gods; particularly fascinating is the way they adopt even the spiritual natures of their namesakes. *Eye Of Cat* (1982) compellingly mixes sf elements and Navajo Indian beliefs in a tense thriller which explores identity and the nature of the hunter. Zelazny is also noted for his short stories, for example 'He Who Shapes' (in *The Last Defender Of Camelot*, 1980), the story of a powerful but flawed psychiatrist in a future where patients are cured by artificial dreams under his control. *Nine Princes In Amber* (1972) is the opening book of the Amber series. Its hero, Corwin, wakes amnesiac in a hospital on Earth, and embarks on a quest first for his identity and then for the throne of Amber, the master-world of which ours is but a shadow. Like many of Zelazny's protagonists, Corwin is an immortal, physically and mentally far superior to ordinary humanity, but cursed with arrogance and pride. During the series his gradual acquisition of self-knowledge parallels the reader's increasing appreciation of the marvels of Amber and her mysterious enemies.

READ·ON   ● *The Doors Of His Face, The Lamps Of His Mouth* (collection)
                Jack Of Shadows
                Dilvish The Damned
              ▶ ▷ C J Cherryh, *Gate Of Ivrel*
                ▷ Philip José Farmer, *Maker Of Universes*
                Alan Moore with Dave Gibbons, *Watchmen* (graphic novel)

Index

Page references in **bold type**
indicate an author main entry